DISCARD Totally Kosher

Totally Kosher

Tradition with a twist!
150+ recipes for the holidays and every day

Chanie Apfelbaum

Photographs by Chanie Apfelbaum

Clarkson Potter/Publishers
New York

Macaroni Salad
4-5 tbs mayonaise
4 tbs ving or lemon
2-3 tbs sugar
1-2 water
1-2 cup green pepper
1/2 cup onion chopped
1/2 cup carrot.

Blintz
frozen bleny
6 egg
Pint of sou
ugar - 1
mon -
anilla -
350° - 1 hr

To the special women in my life who have shaped
me and made me who I am today—

In loving memory of my dear Bubby Hecht, who
taught me that the secret ingredient is love.

To my mother, who instilled in me the greatest
Jewish pride, for showing me the beauty of
celebrating our heritage and traditions through food.

And to my daughters, Chuma, Esther, and Rosie, for
the great privilege of nourishing and nurturing you as
I watch you grow into beautiful young ladies whom
I am so very proud of.

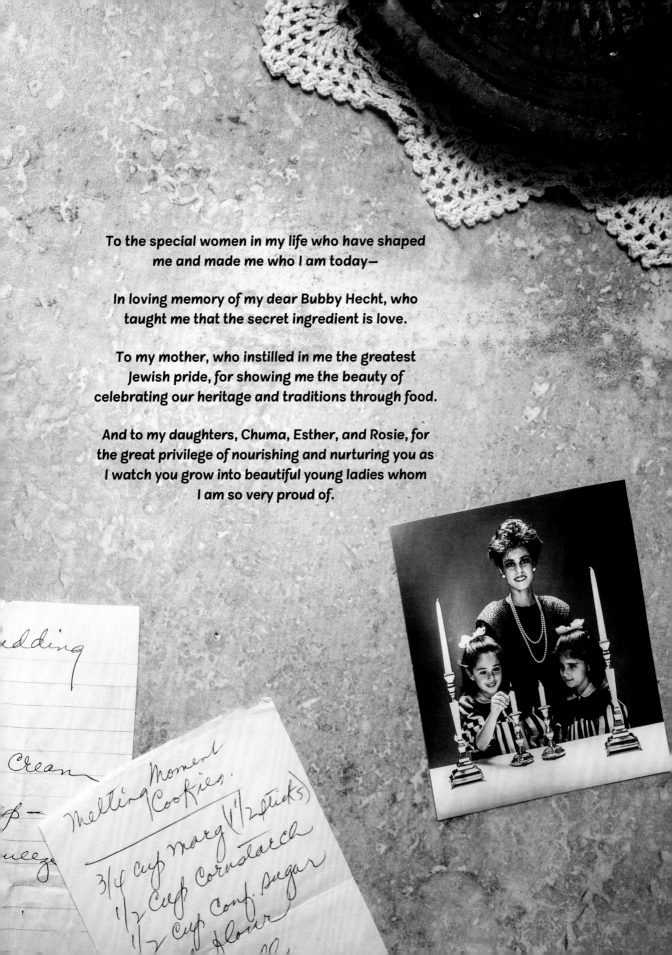

Contents

Split Hooves

Meatless Meals

Veg & Sides

The Bakery

Noshes & Nibbles

You're So Extra!

Introduction

It was January 19, 2011, when I took up *yet another* hobby, a humble blog named *Busy in Brooklyn*, to add to my hodgepodge of avocations. I'd been dillydallying in the arts for years—from scrapbooking to knitting, photography to calligraphy, I had tried them all. With three young children at home, it was time to leave my job as a web designer, but I needed an outlet for my creative energy. I had started sharing some of my birthday cake creations, crochet projects, and simple kosher dinners on Facebook, and the feedback was coming in strong: *start a blog*!

So I went in blind, with no expectations, thinking that my blog would go by the way of my other hobbies, another short-lived stint.

And here I am, twelve years later, a professional food writer and self-taught photographer lucky enough to travel the world sharing what I am so passionate about: bringing families around the table to celebrate our traditions and Jewish pride through food.

What was it about blogging that stuck for me? Well, it certainly wasn't my love of cooking—at least not in the early days. I was one of those newly-marrieds who had never stepped foot in the kitchen, but learning to cook is a rite of passage for a Jewish housewife, so I did what any young bride does—I ordered takeout! Then, on Fridays, when I had to get Shabbat dinner prepped, I'd call my mom and ask for recipes for her traditional gefilte fish, chicken soup, and kugel. *Lots and lots of kugel.*

When I started hosting Shabbat dinners, I realized that cooking didn't have to be a chore. Instead it could be a means for me to express myself creatively. Friends would ooh and aah over my dishes, and it proved the maxim "People eat with their eyes first" to be true. Food started to not seem all that boring anymore—the kitchen became my studio, and my dishes were a blank canvas to explore my artistic side. So I dived in and began binge-watching the Food Network and poring over food blogs and food magazines, and I eventually took a crash course in photography that segued into a full-on kosher culinary school adventure. Before long, that young bride who couldn't cook an egg slowly and steadily learned to hone her skills in the kitchen and behind the camera.

Soon after, I started to receive photos of my recipes out of other people's kitchens—testimony from moms like me who gathered their children around the table for weeknight dinners, messages from novice cooks who baked my challah recipe for the first time for Shabbat, DMs from nonaffiliated Jews celebrating Rosh Hashanah over my brisket recipe—it fueled me and filled me with the greatest sense of purpose.

The feelings run deep for me because, when I was thirteen years old, my oldest brother, Ari Halberstam, was killed in a terrorist attack on the Brooklyn Bridge simply for being Jewish. He was a six-foot-tall, blue-eyed, funny, and charming sixteen-year-old, a star on the basketball court, who took so much pride in his Jewishness. Ari was a prankster, and as his younger sister (and the middle child!), I bore the brunt of his many escapades, but he was also fiercely protective and my biggest champion. Finding a path to honor my brother Ari's memory is the greatest gift of my journey. Every *Busy in Brooklyn* recipe that other families share around a holiday table, every blessing made over one of my kosher creations, and every opportunity to share the love of food, family, and tradition among one another is a means to celebrate what my brother Ari lived and died for. From the depth of my heart, I thank you for giving me the privilege and honor of gracing your holiday tables and for making space for my cookbook on your shelf.

Chanie Apfelbaum

The Kosher Kitchen

When I tell people that I'm a *kosher* food writer, I'm often met with a puzzled look or an interesting question (no, a rabbi doesn't come to my house and bless my food!). So what is kosher anyway?

The popular saying "two Jews, three opinions" is a great way to sum up the kosher conundrum. On the surface, the kosher rules are fairly simple: no pork or shellfish or mixing milk and meat in the same meal or dish. But on a deeper level, it's a lot more complex. Jews of different affiliations and backgrounds adhere to varying degrees of strictness, from keeping kosher "in the house" to eating "kosher-style" or purchasing only kosher-certified ingredients and keeping two separate areas of the kitchen, one for meat and one for dairy (see page 14).

Kosher laws can be restrictive, but they're also an opportunity to get creative and think outside the box. While cooks may not be able to sear a steak in butter, they can use the rich fat from rendered bone marrow; and while cheeseburgers are off-limits, the availability of plant-based meats makes a smash burger easily accessible. In fact, keeping kosher has never been easier. Many ingredients from other cultures around the world are now certified kosher, kosher restaurants abound in resort destinations, and local eateries are broadening their horizons with diverse menus and cuisines.

So, what are the rules really? Well, without getting too technical (because that would require an entire book on the subject!), the laws of "kosher" are derived from the Torah, or Bible, as enumerated in the books of Leviticus and Deuteronomy. The laws were handed down through the generations and eventually expanded on in the Mishnah and Talmud. The Hebrew word *kosher* is defined as "fit," since laws of kosher define the foods that are fit for consumption for a Jew.

THE BASICS OF KEEPING KOSHER

Mammals: must both chew their cud and have split hooves.

Fowl: turkeys, chickens, geese, and ducks are kosher, but not birds of prey.

Fish and seafood: must have fins and scales; no shellfish.

Reptiles, amphibians, worms, and insects: not kosher, aside from four species of locust. Consequently, fruits and vegetables are examined to ensure they are worm- and insect-free.

Since blood represents life, the Torah forbids the consumption of blood, so mammals and fowl must undergo ritual slaughter followed by a soaking and salting process to extract any blood. Eggs are also checked for blood spots before using.

THE SEPARATION OF MILK AND MEAT

One of the basic tenets of keeping kosher is that meat and milk may not be combined. There is a waiting period between eating them, and even separate utensils are used for each. Kosher food is therefore divided into three categories:

Meat: includes the meat or bones of mammals and fowl or any food containing them.

Dairy: includes the milk of any kosher animal and all products made with milk or that contain milk.

Pareve: includes foods that are neutral—neither "meat" nor "dairy," such as eggs from a kosher animal, fruits, vegetables, and grains. These foods may be mixed with or eaten together with either meat or dairy. The only exception is fish. While pareve, the Talmud states that one should not eat it with meat, and some have a custom not to eat it with dairy as well.

As a result of this separation, many kosher observant Jews maintain two separate areas of the kitchen, including separate meat and dairy (and if they're lucky, sometimes even pareve) sinks, ovens, dishwashers (and appliances), as well as separate pots, dishes, utensils, and the like. To avoid confusion, some people purchase color-coded or labeled utensils, typically red for meat, blue for dairy, and green for pareve (see page 12).

You'll find that most of the baked goods in this book use oil instead of butter as the fat. While butter often adds richness and flavor, kosher-keepers would be limited to serving it with dairy meals, so I prefer to keep the recipes pareve.

KOSHER CERTIFICATION

Because of the complexity of kosher laws and the intricacies of modern-day food production, kosher certification is needed for restaurants and for processed foods to ensure that all kosher rules and regulations have been met.

Kosher status is indicated by a symbol, printed on packaging, that represents that the production of the product was under rabbinical supervision and has been certified kosher by the kosher-certifying agency. Restaurants also carry kosher certificates that guarantee that they meet kosher standards.

Jewish Food vs. Kosher Food

SINCE MOST PEOPLE WHO OBSERVE KOSHER ARE JEWISH AND TEND TO COOK traditional Jewish food, it stands to reason that most kosher food is Jewish food. But the same can't be said for Jewish food, which, ironically, is not always kosher. The iconic "Jewish deli" often lists treif (non-kosher) foods on the menu, and many culturally Jewish foods are not inherently kosher. For example, the quintessential Jewish deli sandwich—the Reuben—includes corned beef, Swiss cheese, sauerkraut, and Russian dressing on rye bread, a no-no in the kosher kitchen since it mixes both dairy and meat.

Inasmuch as Jewish cuisine is largely shaped by the laws of kosher, Jewish festivals and customs also help define the foods that we cook and eat. In ritually observant homes, cooking on Shabbat is prohibited, so dishes like cholent (see page 134) and kugel (see page 133) are prepared in advance on Friday afternoon and left to simmer overnight in a slow cooker or on a hot plate. During Passover, it is prohibited to eat chometz, or leavened products, so gluten-free recipes are all the rage, and dishes like my Gluten-Free Scones (page 265) and Matzo Panzanella (page 102) are sure to become holiday staples.

Traditional Jewish foods vary greatly by region and subculture, with Ashkenazi cuisine heavily influenced by the foods of Eastern Europe, while Sephardic cuisine draws its roots from ancient Spain and Portugal. As an "Ashke" girl myself, I include many recipes here that draw from the foods of my youth, but kosher food is not limited to tradition. I live in New York City and love to explore different cuisines, with Korean, Thai, and Middle Eastern being some of my favorites. My Pad Chai (page 156) is one of my most crave-worthy fusion recipes, but I'm also passionate about kosherizing traditionally treif dishes, so kosher-keepers don't have to feel limited in the kitchen. My Philly "Cheesesteak" sandwich (page 71) makes use of meaty portobellos for a kosher spin on the iconic sandwich.

Most of all, I'm here to dispel the myth that kosher food is unhealthy (you won't find margarine in any of my recipes!), heavy (Simply Crudo with Cilantro Crema, page 150, anyone?), and brown (Jeweled Hummus, page 50, FTW!). I'm here to show you that kosher food can be both timeless and modern, simple or sophisticated, healthy or indulgent; it can be traditional or cultural (or both!). Kosher food is good food. Kosher food is comfort food. Kosher food is whatever you want it to be. It's totally kosher.

Top Ten Ingredients to Transform Kosher Cooking

COCONUT MILK (FULL-FAT)

A great nondairy substitute for recipes that call for heavy cream, such as Alfredo sauce, soup, and chocolate ganache. Also a great alternative for healthier whipped cream (see page 253).

COCONUT OIL (REFINED OR EXPELLER PRESSED)

Whether it's solid or liquid, coconut oil is a go-to nondairy substitute for recipes that call for butter. Use for pie crusts, cookies, cakes, chocolate glaze, soups, and curries. For a neutral non-coconutty flavor, look for refined coconut oil—unrefined oil (also called virgin oil) has a strong coconut taste.

CHICKEN BROTH

Broth adds flavor to soups, rice, gravy, stews, and braised meats. It's also my secret to making creamy butter-free mashed potatoes. For pareve dishes, I rely on Imagine No-Chicken Broth. It's organic, with no added MSG or artificial ingredients.

NUTRITIONAL YEAST

Bon Appétit calls it "Nature's Cheeto dust"; I think it's the perfect replacement for Parmesan or cheese in pareve or meat dishes.

TAHINI PASTE

With its high-fat content, tahini (sesame paste) makes a great pareve thickener for soups and pies (Tahini Pumpkin Pie, page 244). It's also a healthy substitute for mayonnaise in dressings (Broccoli Salad 2.0, page 90).

DRIED AND FRESH MUSHROOMS

Mushrooms add umami, or savoriness, to dishes and therefore make a great replacement for meat in pareve dishes like the Philly "Cheesesteak" on page 71.

SOY SAUCE

Soy sauce adds umami and depth to pareve dishes that need a boost of flavor (like Cholent with Quick Kishke, page 134). For a soy-free replacement, use coconut aminos. For a gluten-free replacement, use tamari.

PLANT-BASED MEAT

Plant-based meat has revolutionized kosher cooking. I'm not a big fan of vegan cheese, so when I want to "kosherize" a dish that contains both meat and cheese, I prefer to use plant-based meat and real dairy as opposed to real meat and fake dairy. From smash burgers to meatball subs, meaty lasagne, nachos, or taco pizza, almost nothing is off-limits these days!

MISO PASTE

Miso is a fermented soybean paste that adds depth, complexity, saltiness, and umami to food. It comes in varying degrees of fermentation, with colors ranging from white to red to dark brown. The darker the miso, the stronger and saltier the flavor. White, or shiro, miso is the youngest and sweetest variety. Miso makes a great addition to soup, salad dressings, and marinades for fish, poultry, and meat (Miso London Broil, page 183). It can even be used in sweet applications like chocolate chip cookies or caramel!

MAYONNAISE

Go to any traditional kosher take-out place and you're apt to find thirty different dips that are mayo-based. While overused in Ashkenazi cuisine, I can't disregard its benefits. Mayonnaise makes a great base for nondairy crema, dressings, dips, and sauces. Many commercial brands offer olive oil– or avocado oil–based alternatives that are healthier than the stuff we grew up on.

Top Ten Tools for Your Kosher Kitchen

(SEE PAGE 12)

CHEF'S KNIFE

If salt is the most essential ingredient in the kitchen, a knife is your most essential tool. In many kosher kitchens, you'll find red, blue, and pareve knives for meat, milk, and pareve dishes, but they are mostly paring knives meant for small tasks. I recommend that every cook invest in a good-quality all-purpose chef's knife to properly chop vegetables and break down meat, poultry, and fish. A knife is an extension of your arm, and just as everyone has different-size arms and hands, there's no one size fits all. Try out different shapes and styles (I prefer a santoku knife because the shape and style fit my small hands) to see what you're comfortable with.

BAKING SHEETS

When you need to get dinner on the table every night, Shabbat meals every week, and holidays throughout the year, it's reasonable that many cooks rely on disposable aluminum baking pans for cooking. However, investing in a few real restaurant-grade baking sheets will transform your cooking. Affordable, durable, and easy to clean, sheet pans conduct heat quickly and uniformly. They're great for baking cookies and pastries and for roasting chicken, meat, fish, and vegetables. Half-sheets, which measure 13 × 18 inches, are standard, but I also like to use quarter-sheet pans for toasting nuts, seeds, coconut, and bread crumbs. They're also great for setting up dredging stations for frying.

BAKING RACK

Living in Brooklyn, I don't do much grilling in the winter, so I rely on my broiler for "oven-grilled" chicken and meats. A broiler is like an inverted grill, with the heat source coming from above; you need to position your proteins on a rack set over a baking sheet so the fat can drain as you cook. That's where a wire baking rack comes in. It's the best way to make burgers, cook beef bacon, dehydrate foods, cool baked goods, and keep fried food crisp. Note that *cooling racks* for cookies are not always oven-safe, so make sure to purchase a baking rack that is safe to use at high temperatures.

JULIENNE PEELER

If you have a small kitchen like I do, you probably don't have room for lots of gadgets and gizmos, but a julienne peeler is worth making space for, and it doesn't take up much! It's about the same size as a regular peeler but has microblades along the blade so that when you peel vegetables, it slices them into julienne strips. I use it to julienne carrots for ramen, cucumbers for salads, zucchini for zoodles, or potatoes for hash browns.

Y PEELER

A standard Y peeler works great for shaving radishes and carrots (slice on the bias and then peel against it). You can also create ribbons of zucchini, yellow squash, carrots, parsnips, butternut squash, mango, and avocado. Y peelers are also great for zesting citrus to be used in sauces (so you don't get any pith), shaving chocolate, Parmesan, and even butter.

MICROPLANE

A Microplane (or rasp-style grater) is most often used for zesting citrus, but it's also a great tool for grating garlic into dressings and dips or grating ginger for stir-fries and marinades. It can also be used to grate whole spices like cinnamon, nutmeg, or star anise for desserts and Parmesan or nuts (try grating pine nuts as a Parmesan substitute for pareve!) for savory dishes.

ICE CUBE TRAY

Ice cube trays are for so much more than ice! Use them to freeze coffee for coffee ice cubes (so you don't water down your iced coffee), pesto, leftover tomato paste, wine, stock for sauces, caramelized onions, fresh herbs in olive oil, chipotle chiles in adobo, leftover canned coconut milk, and citrus zest or juice.

SPIDER

A spider is used to drain and remove foods from hot oil, stock, and boiling water. It's also great for skimming soups and stocks, blanching vegetables, and deep-frying foods, from dumplings to donuts and vegetables. Instead of draining pasta or gnocchi into a colander, remove it with a spider so you can reserve the pasta water.

MINI FOOD PROCESSOR

Food processors can be bulky and take up a lot of space, but a mini one is worth the investment. Before Shabbat or holiday cooking, I use it to mince a few heads of garlic at a time. It's also great for mincing herbs, mincing onions for meatballs, whipping up a dressing, or chopping nuts.

ICE CREAM SCOOP

Ice cream scoops are great for portioning out batter for cupcakes or muffins, pancakes, cookie dough, meatballs, patties, or latkes. It's also great for removing seeds from squash and melons (you can even use it to make melon balls!).

Top Ten Kitchen Hacks

KEEPING YOUR FOOD PROCESSOR CLEAN

Probably my favorite hack of all time, I use this one daily! When using your food processor, cover the bowl with plastic wrap before putting the lid on. It will keep the lid clean when blending. (Don't do this if you plan to pour oil or anything through the spout. Ask me how I know! LOL).

MELTING CHOCOLATE

My second most favorite hack! To melt chocolate, place chocolate chips in a resealable freezer Ziploc® bag, and hold the bag so the chips consolidate into one corner. Place the pointed tip of the bag in a mug (you can let the rest of the sealed portion hang over the side), and pour boiling water over it so the chocolate is fully submerged (see photo, at right). Let the chocolate melt for 2 minutes, then remove the bag from the water and massage it. Return to the water for an additional 2 minutes, until fully melted. Snip the corner of the bag and drizzle the chocolate!

JUICING LIMES

To get the juices flowing in your limes, roll and press it on a hard surface. Halve and place it cut-side down between a pair of tongs, hold over a bowl, and press the tongs closed to squeeze out the juice. Repeat with the remaining half.

DESEEDING A POMEGRANATE

Cut the pomegranate in half around its equator, and remove the crowned tip from the top half of the pomegranate. Over a bowl, gently press the skin to loosen the seeds from the membranes. Hold half of the pomegranate open facedown in the palm of your hand, and with a heavy spoon or mallet, tap the pomegranate. You will see the seeds start to fall out. Continue tapping the pomegranate all around, on all sides, until all the seeds have released. Repeat with the remaining half of the pomegranate.

SOFTENING BUTTER

To soften a stick of butter quickly, cut the butter into small pieces, grate with a box grater, or shave with a peeler.

FLAVORED ICE CUBES

Instead of watering down drinks with regular ice cubes, use frozen grapes or the fruit of your choice, frozen coffee cubes or frozen milk cubes for iced coffee, or cubes of frozen wine for sangria.

THINLY SLICING MEAT, POULTRY, AND FISH

To thinly slice meat for jerky (see page 279) or pho, poultry for stir-fry, or fish for crudo (see page 150), partially freeze the protein for 1 to 2 hours before slicing.

RESERVING CHICKEN TENDERS

To get the most bang for your buck, before cooking a chicken breast, remove the flap of meat from its underside, place it in a resealable ziptop plastic bag, and freeze. When you have a few bags, use the tenders for chicken soup, stir-fry, or schnitzel.

DISCARDING CHICKEN OR BEEF FAT

To discard rendered chicken or beef fat, line a bowl with foil and pour the fat into the bowl. Place in the fridge or freezer until solid and then discard.

ALWAYS SPREADABLE NUT BUTTER

If your nut butter or tahini tends to separate, store it upside down to redistribute the oils.

My favorite hack for melting chocolate!

Cheese Board,
page 22

Top Ten BYOB (Build Your Own Boards)

I'll use any excuse to build a board—whether it's for a fun weeknight dinner with my kids (I always say that the best way to get kids to eat is to give them choices—when they get to build their own plate, they feel in control and they're much more likely to try new foods!), a Shabbat lunch, or an appetizer before a holiday feast, board building is a fun and easy way to serve an entire course, from appetizers to desserts. The great part about serving food on a board is that most of the components are often store-bought, so it's really just about assembly—yet it's still a showstopping feast for the eyes!

To build a board, you'll need a large rustic wood or marble board to act as the platter. Then follow these basic rules:

- Use an assortment of colors and shapes to create visual interest, and arrange the ingredients in a free-form style. Incorporate small bowls and dipping cups between items. These can hold any of the condiments listed below.

- Incorporate different textures and flavors onto the board: something sweet, salty, acidic, creamy, crunchy, and sticky.

CHOOSE FROM THESE CATEGORIES

Protein: cheese, charcuterie, fish, Hard-Boiled Eggs (page 293)

Fresh and / or Dried Fruit: whole or sliced

Vegetables and Herbs: look for minis and stem-on, like radishes and carrots

Pickles and Olives: Pomegranate Pickled Onions (page 292), Candied Jalapeños (page 292), cornichons, peppers, radishes, green and / or black olives

Nuts and Seeds: Candied Pecans (page 272), smoked or salted nuts and seeds

Bread and Crackers: breadsticks, sourdough bread, seeded crackers (see page 283)

Condiments: pesto, Sundried Tomato Tapenade (page 300), jam, honey, mustard, Chipotle Aioli (page 300)

Fish Board

(SEE FISH CHAPTER PHOTO, PAGE 138)

My go-to for Sunday brunch, Shabbat lunch, and holiday feasts

whole smoked white fish • gravlax • herring • white fish dip or tuna salad • Hard-Boiled Eggs (page 293) • tomatoes on the vine • cucumber slices • radishes • jalapeño peppers • capers • cornichons • olives • pickled or sliced red onion • lemon slices • crackers (see page 283) • fresh dill • herbed mayo or cream cheese

Sushi Board

I serve this on a lazy Susan with the rice in the middle

sushi rice (see page 40) • flaked cooked salmon or sushi-grade tuna cubes • shredded kani (imitation crabmeat) • cucumber slices • julienned carrot • radish • cubed avocado • shelled edamame • cubed mango • freshly chopped chives • pickled ginger • french-fried onions • nori • toasted sesame seeds • spicy mayo • kosher eel sauce (sweet sauce) • wasabi • sriracha

Cheese Board

A cheese board should incorporate "something old, something new, something goat, something blue"—an aged cheese, a fresh cheese, a goat cheese, and a moldy cheese!

aged Cheddar • wedge of parmesan • feta cubes or ciliegine marinated in herbs and olive oil • goat cheese rolled in Everything Bagel Spice (page 305), herbs, or edible flowers • Brie or Camembert • grapes • berries • apple or pear slices • dried or fresh figs • dried apricots or dates • pomegranate halves or arils • radishes • tomatoes on the vine • olives • cornichons • candied pecans (see page 272) • smoked almonds • jam • guava paste • pesto • honeycomb • crackers • breadsticks

Charcuterie Board

An easy Shabbat lunch board with any deli or proteins you have on hand

sliced London broil (see page 183) or corned beef • hasselback salami (see page 65) • smoked turkey • beef jerky (see page 279) • chicken liver pâté • franks in blanks • grapes • pickles • olives • Pomegranate Pickled Onions (page 292) • tomatoes on the vine • dried dates • dried figs • almonds • assorted mustards • Chimichurri (page 301) • jam • crackers • smoked salt

Taco Board

A fun way to embrace Taco Tuesday!

taco spiced ground beef / London broil (see page 183) / skirt steak (see page 85) / pulled beef (see page 188) / refried beans • red cabbage slaw (see page 98) • shredded lettuce • diced tomato • sliced red onion • corn • avocado (guacamole) • Pomegranate Pickled Onions (page 292) or Candied Jalapeños (page 292) • soft corn tortillas • hard taco shells • vegan sour cream • salsa • cilantro

Baked Potato Board

A weeknight dinner my kids and I adore!

baked potatoes • baked sweet potatoes • vegetarian chili or baked beans • tuna salad (see page 75) • steamed broccoli • fresh corn • avocado • sliced red onion • Candied Jalapeños (page 292) • scallions • salsa • sour cream • Cheddar cheese sauce

Falafel Board

Meatless Monday never looked so good!

mini pitas • Smashed Falafel (page 202) • fried or roasted eggplant (see page 98) • Hard-Boiled Eggs (page 293) • red cabbage slaw (see page 98) • Israeli Salad (see page 62) • roasted chickpeas (see page 62) • pickled beets • pickled turnips • preserved lemons • Israeli pickles • pickled hot peppers • hummus (see page 50) • Extra-Creamy Tahini (page 301) • Smoky

Fish Board, page 22

Harissa (page 303) • Schug (page 301) • amba • Sumac Onions (page 62) • sauerkraut • parsley

BBQ Board

Great for BBQ season all summer—and winter—long.

burgers (see page 179) • grilled hot dogs • steak (see page 180) • crispy beef bacon (see page 179) • sunny-side-up eggs • toasted buns • corn on the cob • shredded lettuce • sliced tomato • sliced red onion • pickles • sauerkraut • mustard • ketchup • BBQ sauce • Special Sauce (page 179)

Breakfast Board

(SEE BREAKFAST CHAPTER PHOTO, PAGE 28)

I love to serve this on a quarter-sheet tray, Israeli-style, with a little bit of everything you have on hand.

eggs, any style • toast • seasonal salad • labneh • assorted cheeses • tapenade (see page 300) •

pesto • tuna salad (see page 75) • Israeli pickles • pickled hot peppers • fresh fruit • halva • jam • yogurt • granola • pastry

Dessert Board

When you haven't made dessert but you want to serve an after-dinner treat, just throw a board together!

sliced babka • halva chunks • after-dinner-mints • jelly rings • wafer rolls • biscuits • strawberries • grapes • berries • dried fruit • candied nuts (see page 272) • pretzels (see page 275) • popcorn • whipped cream • cookie butter • chocolate spread

How I Master Dinner, Every Day of the Week

When it comes to putting food on the table, I have to admit that I'm not much of a planner, which is a bit crazy since I have five kids. I like to keep things fresh and exciting, so a weekly or biweekly rotation doesn't really do it for me. But without a schedule, dinner can be daunting. So I narrowed it down to this basic schedule. It gives me parameters, so I don't feel overwhelmed, while still leaving room for creativity and spontaneity.

Sunday: Leftovers or takeout
Monday: Meatless
Tuesday: Beef
Wednesday: Chicken
Thursday: Dairy
Friday: Shabbat dinner
Saturday Night: Eggs

Sundays

Typically a family day, I don't want to have to think about what's for dinner. If there are leftovers from Shabbat, that's the best-case scenario; otherwise, if we are out for the day, we'll go to a restaurant, or if I'm tired, we'll order takeout. It's important to show yourself grace!

Mondays

After a long weekend of animal protein, we are ready for a break! I usually cook up some vegan fare like refried beans, curry (see page 201), or falafel (see page 202). Sometimes we'll go pescatarian with fish and chips (see page 146) or sushi bowls (see Sushi Board, page 22).

Tuesdays

We love Taco Tuesday, but we don't always stuff our meat into a taco. Sometimes we use it to make spaghetti Bolognese (see page 176), meatballs (see page 192), steak (see page 180) and mashed potatoes, burgers (see page 179), or sausage and peppers.

Wednesdays

I'll often throw everything—chicken and vegetables—on a sheet tray for a one-pan meal (see page 160). We also love pulled chicken sandwiches, chicken ramen bowls, and chicken stir-fry. If I forget to take chicken out of the freezer, I place it—still frozen—in the pressure cooker—works like a charm (see page 159)!

Thursdays

We keep it simple with mac 'n' cheese, baked ziti, grilled cheese paninis, or breakfast for dinner—French toast, waffles (see page 39), or pancakes (see page 31) with all the fixings. If it's been a long week, I order pizza!

Fridays

There's nothing like Friday night dinner. After a long week, we unplug, light the Shabbat candles, and sit around the table sharing stories about our week. My menu is never quite the same, but it usually includes challah (see page 127) with a salad and some dips (see page 302), chicken soup (see page 131), and chicken or meat with roasted vegetables and sides.

Saturday Nights

After a hearty Shabbat lunch, we like to keep things light with some scrambled egg tacos, shakshuka (see page 218), or malawach with Hard-Boiled Eggs (page 293), Resek (page 301), and Schug (page 301).

Turkey Roast with Za'atar Gravy (page 172), Za'atar Smashed Brussels Sprouts (page 233), Cranberry Sauce from Pucker Up Ribs (page 187), Tahini Pumpkin Pie (page 244)

Recipe Notes

Oils

All recipes in this book use extra-virgin olive oil and refined coconut oil unless otherwise specified. For some salad dressings and high-heat cooking, I prefer grapeseed oil because of its neutral flavor and high smoke point, but you may replace it with canola or avocado oil.

Eggs

All recipes in this book use extra-large eggs unless otherwise specified. Since blood spots render eggs unfit for the kosher kitchen, I prefer not to purchase brown eggs (they almost always have blood spots!), and the standardized eggs in my neighborhood kosher supermarket are all XL! Large eggs can be easily substituted in almost all the recipes.

Salt

All recipes in this book use Diamond Crystal kosher salt unless otherwise specified.

Pepper

For recipes that use a large amount of pepper, I prefer to use a coarsely pre-ground pepper; otherwise, I always use freshly ground.

Breakfast & Brunch

Knafeh Pancakes

Makes 10 pancakes

Knafeh is a traditional Middle Eastern dessert made with kataifi (shredded phyllo dough) that is filled with mozzarella cheese, fried or baked, and then soaked in sugar syrup. There are countless versions of this decadent dessert (depending on its country of origin), but they are almost all labor-intensive. This simple, kid-friendly version is my spin on the sweet cheese latkes my mother used to make for us on holidays and special occasions. It's a breakfast worthy of Sunday brunch.

1½ cups sugar, divided
1 tablespoon rosewater
1½ cups all-purpose flour
1½ teaspoons baking powder
½ teaspoon kosher salt
3 extra-large eggs
1 cup whole milk
1 teaspoon pure vanilla extract
1½ cups ricotta or whipped cottage cheese
10 tablespoons unsalted butter
8 ounces frozen kataifi pastry, thawed
Crushed toasted pistachios, for serving
Rose petals, for serving (optional)

1. First, make the rosewater syrup: In a small saucepan over medium heat, combine 1 cup of the sugar and ½ cup water. Bring to a gentle simmer and stir to dissolve the sugar. Simmer for 5 minutes. Remove from the heat and stir in the rosewater. Set aside.

2. In a large bowl, whisk the flour, remaining ½ cup sugar, baking powder, and salt. In a medium bowl, whisk together the eggs, milk, and vanilla. Add the egg mixture to the flour and use a spoon to stir just until combined (do not overmix). Add the ricotta and stir just until incorporated.

3. In a medium nonstick skillet over medium heat, melt 1 tablespoon of the butter until sizzling. Add about ⅓ cup of the kataifi pastry to the skillet so that it's tightly packed into a 4-inch circle (cover the remaining kataifi with a kitchen towel so it doesn't dry out). Pour ⅓ cup pancake batter over the pastry, spreading it out with a spoon, if needed, and cook 5 minutes, until the kataifi is deeply browned and crisp and bubbles start to appear on the surface of the pancake. Use a spatula to flip the pancake over and cook another 2 minutes, until lightly browned. Transfer the pancake to a plate and repeat with the remaining kataifi and pancake batter, adding a tablespoon of butter to the pan for each pancake.

4. To serve, top the pancakes with crushed pistachios and rose petals (if using) and drizzle with the rosewater syrup.

Peanut Butter–Banana Muffins with Oat Streusel

Makes 16 to 18 muffins

This recipe combines some of my favorite breakfast foods—oats, peanut butter, and bananas—into one easy, portable muffin that I can grab on the go! If you have peanut allergies in the house like I do, you can use tahini, almond butter, or any other nut butter (or make these at a friend's house, store them in their freezer, and invite yourself over for coffee when you want one!).

STREUSEL

¾ cup old-fashioned rolled oats

⅔ cup all-purpose flour

⅓ cup packed dark brown sugar

⅓ cup canola oil

½ teaspoon ground cinnamon

½ teaspoon kosher salt

MUFFIN BATTER

1½ cups all-purpose flour

1 teaspoon baking soda

1 teaspoon kosher salt

¼ teaspoon ground cinnamon

3 large, very ripe bananas, finely mashed with a fork (about 1⅓ cups)

2 extra-large eggs

½ cup canola oil

⅓ cup creamy peanut butter (I use Skippy's Natural), plus more (optional) for topping

¼ cup packed dark brown sugar

¼ cup honey

⅓ cup oat milk (or unsweetened milk of choice)

1 teaspoon pure vanilla extract

1. Fill cupcake tins with liners and set aside. Preheat the oven to 350°F with the rack in the middle position.

2. To make the streusel: In a medium bowl, mix together the rolled oats, flour, brown sugar, oil, cinnamon, and salt with a spoon until crumbly and set aside.

3. To prepare the muffins: In a large bowl, whisk together the flour, baking soda, salt, and cinnamon until well-combined.

4. In a separate medium bowl, whisk together the mashed bananas, eggs, oil, peanut butter, brown sugar, honey, oat milk, and vanilla until creamy. Pour the banana mixture into the flour mixture and stir with a spoon to combine.

5. Fill the muffin cups three-quarters full (I like to use a ¼-cup ice cream scoop) and top each with a heaping tablespoon of streusel crumbs. Bake for 20 minutes, or until a toothpick inserted into the center of one comes out clean. Remove the muffins to a wire rack to cool.

6. If desired, warm additional peanut butter in the microwave and drizzle over the muffins.

Freezer-Friendly

Crispy Kale and Egg Skillet for One

I love me some crispy kale chips, especially when baked with nutritional yeast for a cheesy flavor. So I turned it into a breakfast dish because … #putaneggonit makes everything better! This recipe easily doubles to serve more!

1 tablespoon extra-virgin olive oil
2 cups curly kale, stems removed
Kosher salt to taste
½ cup shredded mozzarella
2 extra-large eggs
Sriracha to taste

1. In a 10-inch nonstick skillet over medium heat, heat the olive oil. Add the kale and cook for 5 minutes, or until wilted. Season with salt.

2. Sprinkle the mozzarella around the pan, filling in the nooks and crannies with cheese (these will crisp up into little nuggets of heaven while the eggs cook!).

3. Using a wooden spoon, make two wells in the mixture. Crack the eggs into the wells. Cover the skillet with foil or a lid and cook over medium heat for 3 minutes, or until the egg whites are set but the yolks are still runny.

4. Drizzle sriracha over the eggs and kale, and eat straight from the skillet!

Chocolate Cherry Granola

Makes 5 to 6 cups

I never met a granola I didn't like—and not just for topping my yogurt!
I love to snack on it like trail mix, sprinkle it over ice cream, or eat it like cereal
with milk. This combo of chocolate, cherries, and almonds is so decadent that it
almost feels like dessert. If you can have breakfast for dinner, then why can't
you have dessert for breakfast, am I right?!

½ cup coconut oil (preferably refined)

½ cup maple syrup

3 tablespoons Dutch-process cocoa powder

1 teaspoon kosher salt

1 teaspoon pure vanilla extract

¼ teaspoon ground cinnamon

1½ cups puffed Kamut cereal (or puffed cereal of your choice)

1½ cups old-fashioned rolled oats

1 cup sliced raw almonds

½ cup dried cherries or cranberries

½ cup chopped good-quality dark chocolate

1. Preheat the oven to 350°F. Line a baking sheet with parchment paper.

2. In a large saucepan, melt the coconut oil with the maple syrup over medium-low heat. Remove from the heat and stir in the cocoa, salt, vanilla, and cinnamon. Add the puffed cereal, oats, and almonds and stir until evenly coated.

3. Spread the mixture out on the prepared baking sheet and bake for 20 minutes, stirring halfway through, until the mixture is fragrant, toasted, and darkened. Cool completely. Stir in the dried cherries and chocolate and store in an airtight container for up to 1 month.

Bubby's Challah Kugel, Waffled

Makes 5 waffles

One of the most nostalgic Shabbat foods of my youth is my Bubby's cinnamon-flecked challah kugel. It was sweet and doughy and nothing at all like bread pudding, which seems to be how everyone makes challah kugel these days. Bubby made hers by soaking leftover challah in water and squeezing it out to create a mushy base that she would repurpose into kugel by adding eggs, cinnamon, and sugar. Sounds weird, I know, but believe me, it's the only way to get that pillowy texture. Last summer, I tried waffle-ironing the mixture instead of baking it into kugel, and it was a total delight! The waffle iron crisped up the kugel around the edges, and my kids just loved it. I often make this when I have a leftover loaf of challah.

1 large leftover day-old challah (1 pound)

2 extra-large eggs, beaten

½ cup granulated sugar

¼ cup canola oil, plus more for the waffle iron

1 teaspoon pure vanilla extract

¼ teaspoon ground cinnamon

Pinch of kosher salt

Maple syrup, for serving (optional)

Cinnamon-Sugar (page 305), for sprinkling

1. Remove the crust from the challah and pull the bread apart into palm-size chunks. In a large bowl, cover the bread with room temperature water. Soak just until moistened (not falling apart), 1 minute, and then drain in a colander, pressing down on the challah to draw out as much moisture as possible. Return the challah to the bowl.

2. Mash the wet challah with a potato masher until it resembles mashed potatoes. Add the eggs, sugar, oil, vanilla, cinnamon, and salt and stir to combine.

3. Heat a waffle iron and brush with oil. Add ⅓ cup of the batter and cook for 5 minutes, or until the waffles are browned and crispy and pull away from the waffle iron. Remove it from the waffle iron and transfer to a serving plate. Repeat with the remaining batter.

4. Serve warm, with maple syrup (if using), dusted with Cinnamon-Sugar.

Tahdig Toast with Herb-Whipped Feta and Harissa Eggs

Serves 6

I have never quite mastered the art of tahdig. You know—that gorgeously browned and crispy Persian rice you've likely seen all over your social media feeds! So here's my cheater's version using sticky sushi rice! These crispy bites make a great bed for avocado toast (with Soy-Marinated Eggs [page 293] and Chili Crisp [page 294]), tuna tartare (see page 40), or pulled beef (see page 188).

TAHDIG TOAST
1 cup sushi rice
1 tablespoon unseasoned rice vinegar
1½ teaspoons sugar
½ teaspoon kosher salt
Canola oil, for frying

HERBED WHIPPED FETA
6 ounces feta cheese
2 ounces Greek yogurt
3 tablespoons chopped fresh herbs
   (I use parsley, cilantro, and mint)
1 garlic clove
¼ cup extra-virgin olive oil
Zest and juice from ½ lemon
Pinch of kosher salt
Freshly ground black pepper to taste

HARISSA EGGS
4 tablespoons extra-virgin olive oil
2 tablespoons harissa
6 extra-large eggs

Za'atar and greens or herbs of your choice,
   for serving (optional)

1. To make the tahdig toast: In a sieve, place the sushi rice and rinse under running water until the water runs clear; drain well. Transfer to a saucepan with 1½ cups fresh water. Bring the water and rice to a boil over high heat. Reduce the heat to low, cover with a tight-fitting lid, and simmer for 20 minutes, or until all the liquid is absorbed.

2. In a small bowl, combine the vinegar, sugar, and salt and stir with a spoon to combine.

3. Place the cooked rice in a wide, shallow glass bowl. Using a plastic spoon, toss the rice gently with the vinegar mixture until well dispersed. Let cool completely.

4. In a 10-inch nonstick frying pan, heat the canola oil over high heat. With wet hands, shape the rice into 6 patties, about ½ inch thick. Fry the patties in batches over medium-high heat for 5 minutes, or until a crispy brown crust has formed on the bottom. Flip over to crisp and brown the other side, another 5 minutes. Remove from the pan to a paper towel–lined plate and set aside.

5. To make the herb-whipped feta: In the bowl of a food processor fitted with the S blade, blend the feta, yogurt, herbs, garlic, olive oil, lemon zest and juice, salt, and pepper until whipped and creamy.

6. To make the harissa eggs: In a large skillet over medium heat, heat 2 tablespoons of the olive oil and 1 tablespoon of the harissa in the skillet and stir with a spoon. Crack 3 of the eggs into the skillet and cook for 1 minute, until the whites start to set. Cover and continue cooking 2 to 3 more minutes, until the whites are fully cooked. Remove from the pan and transfer to a plate. Wipe out the skillet and continue with the remaining olive oil, harissa, and eggs.

7. To serve, top the toast with the feta and eggs. Finish with za'atar and greens or herbs of your choice, if desired.

Super Seed Mixed Nut Butter

Makes 16 ounces (about 2 cups)

I hoard nuts in my freezer like no one's business! Cold temperatures keep the nuts from going rancid. I just toast them for optimum freshness. Sometimes, when the freezer gets too full and I need to make space, I'll whip up some homemade nut butter, which is as simple as whizzing the nuts in a food processor until smooth and creamy. I make homemade chocolate-hazelnut spread, gingerbread pecan butter, and salted chocolate walnut butter, but my all-time favorite is actually mixed nut butter—I love how the flavors come together, and the seeds offer incredible texture and crunch (plus, there's more room in the freezer when I use those up too!). Don't worry about measurements here; they're just a suggestion.

1 pound assorted raw nuts, such as almonds, pecans, hazelnuts, and cashews (about 3½ cups)

1 teaspoon kosher salt, or to taste

2 teaspoons hemp seeds

2 teaspoons chia seeds

2 teaspoons flax seeds

1. Preheat the oven to 350°F.

2. Spread the nuts on a parchment-lined baking sheet and bake for 15 to 20 minutes, until they are toasted and fragrant.

3. Transfer the nuts to the bowl of a food processor fitted with the S blade. Add the salt and blend until smooth and creamy, scraping down the sides of the bowl with a rubber spatula as needed (this can take a few minutes, depending on your machine's power).

4. Transfer the nut butter to a 16-ounce glass jar. Stir in the hemp, chia, and flax seeds and mix with a spoon until evenly distributed.

5. Cover and refrigerate for up to 1 month.

6. Serving suggestions: Spread the nut butter on toast and drizzle with honey or jam; sandwich between crackers; use as a dip for pretzels; spread over apples or bananas; drizzle into yogurt.

Bloody Mary Pickled Salmon, page 55

Appetizers & Finger Food

Fried Cornichons with Sweet Chili Dip

Serves 6 to 8

I am a pickle girl and I don't think I've ever met a pickle I didn't like. But if I had to choose one all-time favorite, it would be cornichons, essentially teeny tiny gherkins. First of all, I love little things and anything mini size. But aside from aesthetics, the bite on these is totally sublime! Whenever I order fried pickles at a restaurant, they never quite do it for me because they're always kind of mushy inside, but with cornichons, it's all about the crunch! And with the sweet, tangy, and smoky chili dip for dunking, well, just watch them disappear from the table!

PICKLES

½ cup all-purpose flour

Kosher salt and freshly ground black pepper to taste

3 extra-large eggs, beaten

1½ teaspoons Dijon mustard

1½ teaspoons Frank's RedHot sauce

1½ cups unseasoned panko bread crumbs

1½ teaspoons smoked paprika

1½ teaspoons dried parsley

¾ teaspoon ground cumin

1 (24.3-ounce) jar cornichons, drained

2 cups canola oil, for frying

SWEET CHILI DIP

½ cup mayonnaise

⅓ cup store-bought sweet chili sauce

2 tablespoons ketchup

1 teaspoon freshly squeezed lemon juice

1 teaspoon smoked paprika

¼ teaspoon ground cayenne pepper

Kosher salt to taste

1. To prepare the pickles, first set up a dredging station: In a gallon-size zip-top bag, combine the flour, salt, and pepper. In a shallow bowl, whisk together the eggs, mustard, hot sauce, and some salt and pepper. In a second shallow bowl, combine the panko, paprika, dried parsley, cumin, salt, and pepper.

2. Place the drained cornichons in the bag of flour, seal, and shake until the cornichons are evenly coated. Remove the pickles from the bag with your fingers (see Tip), shaking off the excess flour, and dip them into the eggs, letting the excess egg drip off before placing the pickles in the panko mixture and coating them well on all sides.

3. In a 10-inch skillet over medium-high heat, heat the oil until it reaches 350°F. Line a plate or baking sheet with paper towels and set aside.

4. So as not to overcrowd the pan, fry the panko-coated pickles in batches, 1 minute for each batch, or until golden brown. Remove the fried pickles with a spider or slotted spoon and drain on the prepared paper towels. Serve immediately with chili dip on the side.

5. To make the chili dip: In a small bowl, whisk together the mayonnaise, chili sauce, ketchup, lemon juice, paprika, cayenne, and salt. Store any leftovers in an airtight container in the fridge for up to 2 weeks.

Tip

When breading, use one hand for the dry ingredients and the other hand for the wet ingredients so the breading doesn't stick to your fingers!

Variation

You can also serve these with Ranch Dip (page 64) or Chipotle Aioli (page 300).

Garlic Knot Crown with Brie and Tomato Jam

Serves 8

Brie does not get the love it deserves. And before you turn the page, please, puleeease, just try baking it. It's the gooiest, cheese-pull-of-your-dreams, melty deliciousness you will ever have, and when you pair it with garlic bread and tomato jam, it's a totally over-the-top experience.

TOMATO JAM

1 pint grape tomatoes, cut in half

⅓ cup dry white wine

2 sprigs of fresh thyme

1 tablespoon honey

Kosher salt and freshly ground black pepper to taste

GARLIC KNOT CROWN

1 stick (8 tablespoons) unsalted butter, melted

2 garlic cloves, minced

1 teaspoon dried parsley

½ teaspoon dried oregano

¼ teaspoon dried basil

½ teaspoon kosher salt

1 recipe All-Purpose Pizza Dough (page 207)

1 (7-ounce) wheel of Brie or Camembert

1. To make the jam: In a small saucepan, combine the tomatoes, white wine, thyme, honey, salt, and pepper. Bring the mixture to a simmer over medium heat, reduce the heat to low, and cook, stirring occasionally, for 15 to 20 minutes, until the tomatoes are broken down and the mixture is jammy.

2. While the tomato jam cooks, prepare the garlic knot crown: In a small saucepan over medium heat, melt the butter. Add the garlic, parsley, oregano, basil, and salt and stir for 1 minute, until the garlic is softened (do not brown). Remove the saucepan from the heat and set aside.

3. Divide the pizza dough into eight 3-ounce balls (I like to use a kitchen scale for this). On a lightly floured surface, roll each ball into a 9-inch rope and twist it into a loose knot. Brush a 10-inch round oven-safe baking dish with some of the garlic herb butter and place the Brie in the center. Brush the knots generously with garlic butter and place them around the cheese so that they are lightly touching each other. Cover the baking dish with a kitchen towel and let rise in a warm spot for 20 minutes, until puffed.

4. While the dough is rising, preheat the oven to 400°F. Once the dough is done rising, brush with more garlic butter and bake, uncovered, for 35 minutes, until browned.

5. Remove from the oven and brush again with any remaining garlic butter. Top the Brie with the tomato jam and serve immediately.

Tip

To serve this as a centerpiece, line the baking dish with parchment paper before filling it with cheese and dough. Brush the parchment with the garlic butter, and continue as above. After it's baked, use the parchment paper to lift and transfer the garlic knot crown to a cake stand.

Variation

Top with Sundried Tomato Tapenade (page 300) instead of tomato jam.

Jeweled Hummus

Makes about 2½ cups

Hummus is always the appetizer that's finished to the last swipe, and my secret is in the toppings. You can't just put a bowl of hummus on the table, you've got to show it some love! Warm spiced meat (Nachos Bassar, page 62), shawarma chicken or tempeh (see page 205), caramelized mushrooms, soft-boiled eggs (see page 293), or Harissa-Braised Chickpeas (page 229)—they're all ripe for dipping. One of my all-time favorite hummus dishes is the Hummus Simanim recipe I developed for the high holidays (you can find it on my blog), which gave way to this jeweled version, inspired by Persian jeweled rice.

HUMMUS

1 cup good-quality tahini paste, stir if separated

¼ cup plus 1 tablespoon freshly squeezed lemon juice

2 garlic cloves

2 teaspoons kosher salt

½ teaspoon ground cumin

½ teaspoon saffron threads steeped in ¼ cup hot water

½ cup ice water

2 (15.5-ounce) cans chickpeas, rinsed and drained

TOPPINGS

3 tablespoons shelled raw pistachios

3 tablespoons blanched slivered almonds

1 tablespoon grapeseed oil

1 large carrot, peeled and julienned (about 1 heaping cup)

2 tablespoons sugar

Juice of 1 orange

2 tablespoons extra-virgin olive oil

1 large Spanish onion, halved and thinly sliced into half-moons

½ teaspoon kosher salt

¼ teaspoon ground cardamom

¼ teaspoon ground cumin

¼ teaspoon ground turmeric

¼ teaspoon ground cinnamon

3 tablespoons pomegranate seeds (see page 19 for how to seed)

Rose petals, za'atar and olive oil, for garnish (optional)

1. To make the hummus: In the bowl of a food processor fitted with the S blade, purée the tahini, lemon juice, garlic, salt, cumin, saffron, and water until smooth and creamy, scraping down the sides of the bowl with a rubber spatula as needed. While the machine is running, pour the ice water through the feed tube of the food processor. Blend until the mixture is very smooth. Add the chickpeas and continue blending until the mixture is very smooth and creamy. Adjust the seasoning, adding more salt, cumin, or lemon juice if desired. To adjust the consistency, add a bit of ice water at a time until your desired thickness is achieved. Transfer to a storage container and refrigerate until ready to use.

2. To prepare the toppings: Preheat the oven to 350°F. On separate sides of a small baking sheet, place the pistachios and almonds and bake for 8 minutes, or until toasted and fragrant. Set aside.

3. In a 10-inch nonstick skillet over medium heat, heat the grapeseed oil and then add the carrots. Sauté for 5 minutes, stirring constantly, until the carrots soften. Add the sugar and orange juice and continue to sauté for 5 more minutes, or until the liquid reduces to a glaze. Remove the carrots from the skillet onto a plate and use a paper towel to wipe the skillet clean.

4. In the same skillet, heat the olive oil over medium heat and add the onion. Sauté for about 25 minutes, stirring occasionally, until caramelized. Add the salt, cardamom, cumin,

turmeric, and cinnamon and stir for 1 minute, or until fragrant. Remove the skillet from the heat.

5. To assemble the hummus: Spread it into a large shallow bowl, swirling to create a well in the center with the bottom of a spoon. In the well, place the onions, candied carrots, pistachios, almonds, and pomegranate seeds. Garnish with rose petals, za'atar, and olive oil (if using).

Easy Does It!

Use store-bought hummus instead of homemade.

Notes

- *Hummus can be made up to 2 days ahead. Add the toppings right before serving.*
- *You can find edible unsprayed rose petals on Amazon.*

Shlissel Jerusalem Bagels
Makes 1 key-shaped bagel

On the Shabbat following Passover, it's traditional to bake shlissel challah in the shape of a key (*shlissel* means "key" in Yiddish), as an omen for personal redemption, success, and abundance. My mom bakes our actual house key into the challah (of course, we'd scrub it clean and wrap it in foil first!). This version was inspired by one of my favorite breads, the Jerusalem bagel—which is a Middle Eastern bagel that's oval shaped and covered generously in sesame seeds. I shape the dough around three oven-safe ramekins that get baked right into the dough; fill each with my favorite dips and spreads, like Extra-Creamy Tahini (page 301), Resek (page 301), and Schug (page 301); and then rip and dip right at the table.

¾ cup warm water
1 tablespoon sugar
1½ teaspoons active dry yeast
2 cups bread flour, plus more for dusting
2 tablespoons extra-virgin olive oil
1½ teaspoons kosher salt
1 cup raw sesame seeds

FOR DIPPING
Resek (page 301), Schug (page 301), Extra-Creamy Tahini (page 301), labneh, za'atar, or good-quality extra-virgin olive oil

1. In a large bowl, whisk together the warm water, sugar, and yeast. Stir gently with a spoon and let the mixture rest for 5 minutes, or until foamy.

2. To the yeast mixture, add the flour, olive oil, and salt and mix well with a spoon until a rough dough forms.

3. Turn the dough onto a floured surface and knead for 5 to 6 minutes, until the dough is smooth and elastic. Return the dough to the bowl, cover with a kitchen towel, and set aside to rise in a warm spot for 1 hour, or until doubled in size.

4. Punch down the dough in the bowl and divide it into two equal portions. Roll one portion into a 2-foot-long rope. Roll the second portion into a 1¾-foot rope. Remove 6 inches with a knife or bench scraper from the 1¾-foot rope and cut it in half so you have two 3-inch pieces.

5. Add some water to a large bowl and spread the sesame seeds on a baking sheet. Quickly submerge 1 dough rope in the water then roll in the sesame seeds until fully coated on all sides. Set the dough on the baking sheet and repeat with the second rope and two 3-inch pieces of dough.

6. To shape the key: Loop the 2-foot rope as pictured to create the top of the key. Tuck the 1¼-foot rope under the center of the crown and add the two 3-inch pieces to the bottom, pressing them into the dough so they adhere, resembling the teeth of an old-fashioned key.

7. Place one oven-safe ramekin into each of the three key loops, stretching the dough if needed so it wraps around the ramekin securely.

8. Adjust an oven rack to the lowest position and preheat the oven to 400°F. Bake the key on the bottom oven rack for 25 minutes, until deeply golden. Transfer the bagel to a cooling rack.

9. Fill the ramekins with dips and spreads before serving.

RECIPE CONTINUES

Notes

- If you don't have oven-safe ramekins, crunch aluminum foil into three balls and use that to hold the dough's shape. Remove the foil before serving and nestle in small serving dishes for the dips.

- To make traditional Jerusalem bagels, divide the dough into two portions and roll each into a ball. Poke a hole in the center of each ball and use your fingers to stretch them out until you have two elongated bagels. Dip in water and sesame seeds and bake as above.

- To make classic shlissel challah, use the recipe on page 127 and shape as above.

Freezer-Friendly

You can freeze the raw dough, defrost it in the refrigerator, let it rise at room temperature for 1 hour, and bake as above.

Bloody Mary Pickled Salmon

Serves 8

When Bloody Mary meets pickled salmon, you get a showstopping appetizer that's a refreshing change from traditional herring and is such a fun way to start a meal! Serve with crackers.

8 ounces tomato sauce

½ cup apple cider vinegar

⅓ cup honey

2 tablespoons harissa paste (see page 303 or store-bought)

1 teaspoon ground turmeric

2 teaspoons kosher salt

2 pounds skinless, boneless salmon fillets

1 small Spanish onion, halved, thinly sliced into half-moons

2 tablespoons pickling spice

Optional garnishes and accompaniments:
harissa seasoning and freshly squeezed lemon juice, celery sticks, pickles, pimento-stuffed olives, lemon wedges

1. In a 3-inch-deep skillet, combine the tomato sauce, vinegar, honey, harissa paste, turmeric, salt, and 1 cup water and bring to a boil over medium heat. While the brine is cooking, slice the salmon into ¾-inch strips and then crosswise into ¾-inch cubes.

2. Once the brine is boiling, remove the skillet from the heat and add the salmon, onions, and pickling spice. Give it a gentle stir to ensure that the pickling spice and brine are evenly dispersed. Cover the pan with a lid and set aside to cool completely, about 1 hour.

3. Once fully cooled, transfer the salmon and brine to a 2-quart glass jar and refrigerate for 24 hours.

4. If using the harissa seasoning as a garnish, add it to a small dish. Dip the rim of eight jars or glasses into some freshly squeezed lemon juice and then into the harissa seasoning, twisting to ensure an even coating around the rim. Divide

the fish between the glasses. Garnish each glass with a celery stick, pickles or olives, and a lemon wedge. (See photo on page 44.)

Notes

- *Using this method, the fish will be very lightly cooked with a melt-in-your-mouth texture. If you prefer a firmer fish, simmer the fish in the brine over low heat for 3 to 5 minutes before removing it from the heat.*

- *If you don't like biting into the pickling spice, you can wrap it in a piece of cheesecloth and knot it at the top before adding it to the brine. Discard before serving.*

Pulled Kani Flatbread

Serves 6 to 8

One of my side gigs, aside from food writing, food photography, and teaching cooking classes, is hosting *Chopped*-style cooking competitions. I'm always pleasantly surprised by the dishes the teams come up with using the secret ingredients in the basket that I assemble (I don't make it easy!). I'm often rewarded with an awesome idea from a creative competitor. During a special date-night *Chopped* competition, I put crackers, kani, harissa, and roasted beets in the basket, and the young lady made a delicious appetizer using the prebaked flatbread from the pantry. I loved it so much that I brought the idea home and perfected it for you here!

1 tablespoon cornstarch

2 teaspoons toasted sesame oil

3 garlic cloves, minced

1-inch piece fresh ginger, peeled and grated using a rasp-style grater

¼ cup soy sauce

¼ cup honey

2 tablespoons lime juice

1 teaspoon sriracha

16 ounces frozen kani (mock crab), thawed and pulled apart into thin strips

1 prebaked thin pizza crust, such as Brooklyn Bred

Togarashi Aioli (page 300) or spicy mayo (see Easy Does It! below)

2 scallions (white and green parts), chopped, for garnish

3 radishes, julienned, for garnish

1 cup store-bought french-fried onions, for garnish

2 teaspoons Togarashi Seasoning (page 296) or black and white sesame seeds, for garnish

1. Preheat the oven to 400°F.

2. In a small bowl, whisk together the cornstarch with 1 tablespoon water to form a slurry. Set aside.

3. In a 12-inch skillet over medium heat, heat the sesame oil. Add the garlic and ginger and cook for 2 minutes, stirring occasionally, until fragrant but not browned. Add the soy sauce, honey, lime juice, sriracha, and ⅔ cup water and bring to a simmer. Whisk in the cornstarch mixture to incorporate it into the sauce. Simmer for 2 to 3 minutes, until the sauce thickens and coats the back of a spoon. Add the shredded kani, gently stirring with tongs until evenly coated and warmed through, 2 to 3 more minutes.

4. Place the pizza crust on a sheet pan and toast in the preheated oven for 8 minutes, or until lightly crisp.

5. Spread the aioli onto the pizza crust. Top with the kani. Garnish with the scallions, radishes, french-fried onions, and Togarashi Seasoning. Slice into wedges with a pizza cutter or knife before serving.

Easy Does It!

Instead of making your own sauce, use ¾ cup store-bought sweet sauce (kosher mock eel sauce) and store-bought spicy mayo instead of the Togarashi Aioli.

Simanim Potstickers
with Pomegranate Dipping Sauce
Serves 12

Potstickers are the millennial kreplach, traditionally eaten before the fast of Yom Kippur. I fill them with some of the symbolic foods, called *simanim*, that are customary to eat during the High Holidays to symbolize our hopes for a sweet New Year. These foods include leeks, carrots, apples, pomegranates, and honey.

1 pound ground dark meat turkey

1-inch piece fresh ginger, peeled and grated using a rasp-style grater

2 garlic cloves, grated using a rasp-style grater

¼ cup finely chopped leek (white part only)

⅓ cup shredded carrot

¼ cup shredded apple

1 tablespoon soy sauce

2 teaspoons sesame oil

½ teaspoon kosher salt

1 package wonton wrappers (about 40 wrappers)

Canola oil, for frying

DIPPING SAUCE

¼ cup pomegranate juice

¼ cup honey

2 tablespoons soy sauce

1. Grease a baking sheet with cooking spray and set it aside. In a medium bowl, combine the turkey, ginger, garlic, leek, carrot, apple, soy sauce, sesame oil, and salt with your hands.

2. Set a small bowl of water next to your work space. Working with 1 wonton wrapper at a time, add 2 teaspoons of the filling to the center. Using a pastry brush or your finger, brush water around the edge of the wrapper. Fold the dough over the filling into a triangular or half-moon shape and press down the edges to seal. Transfer the dumpling to a baking sheet and repeat with the remaining wrappers and filling.

3. In a large skillet set over medium heat, heat 1 to 2 tablespoons of canola oil. When the oil shimmers, add the potstickers (working in batches so as not to overcrowd the pan) and cook 2 to 3 minutes, or until the bottoms are light golden brown. Carefully pour 3 tablespoons water into the skillet and immediately cover with a tight-fitting lid, being careful to avoid any splatter. Reduce the heat to low and let the dumplings steam for 4 to 5 minutes, until the filling is cooked through inside (the filling should be opaque and no longer pink). Transfer the potstickers to a serving plate and repeat with the remaining potstickers.

4. To make the dipping sauce: In a small saucepan, combine the pomegranate juice, honey, and soy sauce. Bring the mixture to a simmer over medium heat and cook for 10 to 15 minutes, until the sauce thickens and coats the back of a spoon. Serve the sauce with the potstickers.

Tip
This recipe, minus the wonton wrappers, also makes a great turkey burger!

Freezer-Friendly
To prepare ahead of time, shape the potstickers but do not fry them. Freeze them on a baking sheet until solid, transfer them to a gallon-size zip-top bag, and return to the freezer. When ready to serve, cook the potstickers from frozen, adding an extra 5 minutes of steaming for the turkey to cook through. Alternatively, you can boil the potstickers and add them to soup, or steam them in a steaming basket for 10 minutes.

Kishke Dogs
Serves 10

My son Peretz is so in love with hot dogs, he would eat them every night of the week if I let him, but I usually reserve them for a pre-Shabbat treat, when I make "Franks in Blanks" (the kosher name for pigs in a blanket). One week, I wanted to try something different, and I had homemade kishke batter on hand, so this corndog-esque fusion was born.

1 carrot, peeled and roughly chopped
1 celery stalk, roughly chopped
1 small yellow onion, roughly chopped
1¼ cups all-purpose flour
1 cup yellow cornmeal
¼ cup chicken or vegetable stock
3 extra-large eggs
2 teaspoons sugar
2 teaspoons baking powder
1 teaspoon sweet paprika
1 teaspoon kosher salt
½ teaspoon freshly ground black pepper
14 hot dogs or 10 sausages (they tend to be larger), cut in half crosswise
Canola oil, for frying

1. To the bowl of a food processor fitted with the S blade, add the carrot, celery, and onion. Blend until finely ground. Add the flour, cornmeal, stock, eggs, sugar, baking powder, paprika, salt, and pepper and continue to blend until the mixture is very creamy. Transfer the mixture to a tall drinking glass.

2. Push a wooden skewer through the center of each hot dog or sausage (if the skewer is too long to fit in the pot you will use to fry in, cut it to shorten, but leave enough skewer to use as a handle).

3. Fill a 4-quart saucepan with 2 inches of oil. Heat the oil over medium-high heat until a deep-fry thermometer reads 375°F. (If you don't have a deep-fry thermometer, simply put a wooden skewer in the oil, and if the oil bubbles around the skewer, it is ready.)

4. Working with one hot dog at a time, hold the tip of the skewer and dip the hot dog into the glass of batter. Pull the hot dog out and rotate the skewer to let any excess batter drip back into the glass. Carefully place the hot dog into the hot oil and fry two or three at a time, taking care not to overcrowd the pan, for 2 to 3 minutes, until golden and crisp. Transfer the corndogs to a paper towel–lined plate to drain off the excess oil, and then place the dogs on a serving platter. Repeat with the remaining hot dogs. Serve immediately.

Variation
You can also use this batter to deep-fry chicken tenders, chunks of pastrami, or smoked turkey.

Nachos Bassar

Serves 6

Like the classic Middle Eastern dish, hummus bassar—spiced beef–topped hummus—Nachos Bassar is loaded with all of your favorite toppings. Israeli salad takes the place of pico de gallo, Israeli pickles replace pickled jalapeños, and chickpeas replace black beans. It's all doused in a generous amount of tahini, which rivals any nacho sauce IMHO!

SUMAC ONIONS

1 medium red onion, thinly sliced into half-moons
1½ teaspoons ground sumac
Juice of ½ lemon
Kosher salt to taste

ROASTED CHICKPEAS

1 (14-ounce) can chickpeas, rinsed, drained, and patted dry
1½ teaspoons ground cumin
1 tablespoon extra-virgin olive oil
Kosher salt to taste

PITA CHIPS

3 pitas
½ cup extra-virgin olive oil
Kosher salt to taste

SPICED BEEF

1 tablespoon extra-virgin olive oil
1 medium Spanish onion, finely diced
3 garlic cloves, minced
1½ pounds ground beef (not lean)
2 teaspoons ground cumin
1 teaspoon sweet paprika
½ teaspoon ground allspice
½ teaspoon kosher salt
¼ teaspoon freshly ground black pepper

ISRAELI SALAD

1 Persian cucumber, finely diced
1 plum tomato, finely diced
½ small red onion, finely diced
2 teaspoons extra-virgin olive oil
1 teaspoon freshly squeezed lemon juice
Kosher salt and freshly ground black pepper to taste

TOPPINGS

6 mini Israeli pickles, sliced into ¼-inch-thick coins
1 recipe Extra-Creamy Tahini (page 301)
Fresh parsley, chopped, for garnish

Optional toppings: black olives, roasted eggplant (see page 98), Pomegranate Pickled Onions (page 292), Smoky Harissa (page 303), Schug (page 301)

1. Preheat the oven to 400°F.

2. To prepare the sumac onions: In a small bowl, toss the onions with the sumac, lemon juice, and salt. Allow the onions to soften and pickle for at least 20 minutes before serving or transfer them to an airtight container and keep refrigerated for up to 3 days.

3. To prepare the roasted chickpeas: Spread them out on a baking sheet and toss them with the cumin, olive oil, and salt. Bake for 35 to 45 minutes, shaking the pan once or twice during baking, until crispy.

4. To prepare the pita chips: Cut each pita in half horizontally so that you have 6 split full circles. Stack the circles on top of each other and cut into 8 triangles so you have 48 triangles total. Line two baking sheets with parchment paper. Brush the parchment paper with olive oil and place the pita, puffy-side down, on the parchment. Brush the tops of the pitas with more olive oil and season with a generous sprinkling of salt. Bake 10 to 15 minutes, or until browned and crisp.

5. While the pita is baking, make the beef filling: In a large skillet over medium heat, heat the olive oil and add the onion. Sauté for 5 minutes, or until translucent. Add the garlic and continue to sauté for 1 minute, or until fragrant. Add the beef and cook, stirring often and breaking it up with a spoon, for 6 minutes, or until crumbly and no longer pink. Drain the liquid from the pan and return the pan to the stovetop. Add the cumin, paprika, allspice, salt, and pepper. Stir to combine and sauté over medium heat for 2 minutes, or until fragrant.

6. To make the Israeli salad: In a medium bowl, combine the cucumber, tomato, red onion, olive oil, lemon juice, salt, and pepper and stir.

7. To serve, arrange two layers of the pita chips, beef, Israeli salad, chickpeas, pickles, Extra-Creamy Tahini (page 301), and any other toppings you desire. Garnish with parsley. Serve immediately.

Easy Does It!

Use store-bought pita chips and unroasted chickpeas (drain from the can, rinse, and pat dry).

Buffalo Hasselback Salami

Serves 6

Drunken Hasselback Salami will forever be the recipe that put *Busy in Brooklyn* on the map. Almost every kosher deli (worldwide!) sells it today, and I take so much pride in that! Of course, the story goes that my mom used to serve my siblings and me salami sandwiches every Friday afternoon, and one by one, each of us would chuck it down the incinerator chute of our apartment building! So how did I become such a salami snob? Well, when I learned that frying it renders all the fat and crisps up the edges, I was all in! So, of course, I had to offer you a new version that is inspired by buffalo chicken wings.

BUFFALO SALAMI
1 (14-ounce) salami, unsliced
¼ cup (packed) dark brown sugar
⅓ cup Frank's RedHot sauce or other hot sauce
¼ cup honey
Carrot and celery sticks, for serving (optional)
Ranch Dip, for serving (optional)

RANCH DIP
1 cup mayonnaise
1 garlic clove, minced
1 tablespoon chopped fresh chives
    or 1 teaspoon dried
1 tablespoon chopped fresh parsley
    or 1 teaspoon dried
1 tablespoon chopped fresh dill
    or 1 teaspoon dried
1 tablespoon apple cider vinegar
1 teaspoon onion powder
½ teaspoon garlic powder
½ teaspoon kosher salt
¼ teaspoon freshly ground black pepper

1. Preheat the oven to 400°F.

2. To make the buffalo salami: Remove the wrapper from the salami and place it on a cutting board with chopsticks on either side of the salami. Holding the salami down with one hand, slice it into thin ⅛-inch slices (the chopsticks will ensure that you don't slice all the way through).

3. In a small bowl, stir together the brown sugar, hot sauce, and honey until combined. Generously brush the salami with the prepared sauce, making sure to get in between all the slices. Place the glazed salami in a baking dish and bake for 30 minutes, basting with the pan juices every 10 to 15 minutes, or until the salami is browned and crispy around the edges.

4. To prepare the dip: In the bowl of a food processor fitted with the S blade, blend the mayonnaise, garlic, chives, parsley, dill, vinegar, onion powder, garlic powder, salt, pepper, and 1 tablespoon water until smooth (if using dried herbs, add the ingredients to a small bowl and mix with a spoon instead). Transfer the dip to a serving bowl.

5. Serve the salami warm with carrot and celery sticks and the ranch dip on the side.

Sammies & Tacos

Stuffed Boureka Sandwiches

Makes 4 boureka sandwiches

When people ask me what my favorite dish is, I usually answer, "Can you *have* a favorite child?!" Well if I *could* have a favorite child, they would be named "boureka" because this, my friends, is probably it. In fact, the first place I head when I get off the airplane upon landing in Israel is to Giveret Boureka in Machane Yehuda Shuk in Jerusalem for a fully loaded stuffed boureka sandwich. It's not a snack, it's not finger food, it's a MEAL. You pick your boureka (always, *always* potato!), and they stuff it with hard-boiled eggs, tahini, schug, chimichurri, resek, and Israeli pickles on the side. If I ever end up on that show *The Best Thing I Ever Ate* on the Food Network, you know where we're going!

4 russet potatoes, peeled and diced into medium chunks

3 tablespoons unsalted butter

2 garlic cloves, minced

Kosher salt and freshly ground black pepper to taste

2 extra-large egg yolks

2 sheets frozen puff pastry, thawed (Pepperidge Farm recommended)

1 extra-large egg, for egg wash

2 tablespoons raw sesame seeds

4 peeled and sliced hard-boiled eggs (page 293), Extra-Creamy Tahini (page 301), Smoky Harissa (page 303), Schug (page 301), and Israeli pickles and/or pickled hot peppers, for serving

1. Preheat the oven to 400°F. Line a baking sheet with parchment paper.

2. In a large saucepan, cover the potatoes with cold salted water. Bring to a boil then reduce the heat to a simmer and cook for 20 minutes, or until the potatoes are fork-tender. Drain well and place in a medium bowl.

3. Using a potato masher, mash the potatoes until no lumps remain. Stir in the butter, garlic, salt, and pepper and set aside to let the potatoes cool completely. Once the mixture is cool, add the egg yolks and stir until creamy.

4. Unfold one sheet of the puff pastry onto a sheet of parchment paper and roll into a rectangle about 10 × 14 inches. Cut the sheet in half so you have two 5 × 7-inch rectangles. Spread about 1 cup of the potato filling over the short end of the pastry, leaving a 1-inch border. Fold the empty side of the pastry dough over the side with the filling and press down on the edges with a fork to seal tightly. Repeat with the remaining puff pastry and potatoes.

5. In a small bowl, whisk together the egg with 1 tablespoon water to make an egg wash. Brush the bourekas with the egg wash and sprinkle with ½ tablespoon sesame seeds per boureka.

6. Bake for 20 minutes, or until puffed and golden brown.

7. Briefly cool the bourekas and then slice them in half horizontally through the top layer so that it opens like a book. Fill the bourekas with sliced eggs, Extra-Creamy Tahini, Smoky Harissa, and Schug. Serve with Israeli pickles.

Easy Does It!
Buy store-bought bourekas and fill as above, or make your own using instant mashed potatoes.

Freezer-Friendly

Philly "Cheesesteak"

Makes 2 sandwiches

There's just something about the Philly cheesesteak sandwich that made me want to kosherize it—it looks so decadent! Here I use meaty portobellos to stand in for the steak. They make a great replacement. I once made a kosher cheese "burger" with them, and the recipe won second place in a contest from the Mushroom Council of America (you can find the recipe on my blog)!

¼ cup plus 2 tablespoons grapeseed oil, divided

2 tablespoons soy sauce

1 tablespoon Worcestershire sauce

½ tablespoon balsamic vinegar

½ teaspoon smoked paprika

1 garlic clove, minced

3 portobello mushrooms, stems removed and gills scraped out with a spoon

1 large Spanish onion, sliced into ¼-inch-thick half-moons

1 green bell pepper, seeds and veins removed, sliced into ¼-inch-thick half-moons

1 teaspoon Montreal steak seasoning

4 slices provolone or mozzarella cheese

2 hoagie rolls

1. In a gallon-size zip-top bag, combine ¼ cup of the grapeseed oil, the soy sauce, Worcestershire, vinegar, smoked paprika, and garlic. Add the mushrooms to the bag, give it a shake, and marinate at room temperature for 30 minutes.

2. When the mushrooms are almost done marinating, in a large skillet over high heat, heat the remaining 2 tablespoons oil. Add the onion and pepper and sauté for 5 minutes, stirring occasionally, until tender-crisp. Remove from the pan and set aside.

3. Remove the mushrooms from the bag and slice them into ¼-inch-thick strips. Reduce the heat to medium, add the mushrooms, the marinade, 2 tablespoons water, and the Montreal steak seasoning to the pan and sauté, stirring constantly, 6 to 8 minutes, until the mushrooms soften and the liquid thickens to a glaze. Stir the onions and peppers back into the pan.

4. Top the vegetables with the sliced cheese and cover the skillet with a lid over medium heat for 2 minutes, or until the cheese is just melted. Divide the filling equally between the rolls and serve immediately.

Note

If desired, butter and toast the rolls before filling.

Tartare Tostada

Makes 6 tostadas

If you've never fried rice paper wrappers, you are in for a treat! They puff up like magic into the coolest cracker that is light and airy with a great crunch. Topped with tuna tartare, they make a refreshing lunch or light dinner and a super-fun take on Mexican tostadas.

2 tablespoons soy sauce

1 tablespoon honey

2 teaspoons freshly squeezed lime juice

1 teaspoon toasted sesame oil

1 teaspoon sriracha

½ cup shelled edamame, thawed if frozen

1 pound sushi-grade tuna, diced into small pieces

3 rice paper wrappers, cut in half

Canola oil, for frying

Diced avocado, chopped chives, microgreens, Togarashi Aioli (page 300), and Togarashi Seasoning (page 296) or toasted sesame seeds, for topping

1. In a medium bowl, whisk together the soy sauce, honey, lime juice, sesame oil, and sriracha. Add the tuna and stir to evenly coat the fish. Marinate in the fridge for 20 minutes.

2. While the tuna is marinating, prepare the rice paper puffs. Fill a cast-iron skillet or Dutch oven with 1 inch of oil. Clip a deep-fry thermometer to the skillet. Heat over medium-high heat until the thermometer registers 375°F. Line a baking sheet with paper towels.

3. Gently place 1 rice paper half at a time into the oil and fry 3 to 5 seconds, until doubled in size, puffed, crisp, and white. Transfer with a slotted spoon to the prepared baking sheet to drain. Repeat with the remaining rice paper wrappers.

4. To assemble the tostadas, top the fried rice paper with the marinated tuna. Evenly divide the edamame, avocado, chives, and microgreens over the tuna. Drizzle with the Togarashi Aioli and sprinkle with Togarashi Seasoning.

Variations

• *Use fried corn tortillas instead of fried rice paper wrappers.*

• *You can also serve this recipe over fried rice cakes (see Tahdig Toast, page 40).*

• *To serve as a tuna tower, finely dice the tuna and mix with the marinade and 3 tablespoons mayonnaise. Shape into a ring mold, top with microgreens, and serve with chips or crackers.*

Bougie Tuna Bagel

Makes 2 sandwiches

Does a tuna bagel deserve a spot in a cookbook? Why yes, yes, it does. I'll never forget how my DMs BLEW. UP. when I posted an Instagram story about my favorite way to prepare tuna. Personally, I could eat a tuna sandwich every single day, but who knew so many of you felt the same?! This, then, is a love letter to all the tuna lovers out there. A little sweet, a little tangy.

2 (6-ounce) cans solid albacore tuna packed in water, drained well

¼ cup mayonnaise

2 tablespoons pickle relish

2 teaspoons yellow mustard

2 teaspoons freshly squeezed lemon juice

1 scallion (white and green parts), chopped

¼ cup finely diced celery

2 tablespoons Craisins (trust me!), chopped

Kosher salt and freshly ground black pepper to taste

2 bagels of your choice

Honey mustard, sliced red bell pepper, thinly sliced red onion, iceberg lettuce, and potato chips, for serving

1. In a medium bowl, and using gloves, mush the tuna with your fingers so it's well mashed. Add the mayonnaise, pickle relish, mustard, lemon juice, scallion, celery, Craisins, salt, and pepper. Mix with a spoon until the ingredients are incorporated.

2. Cut the bagels in half and spread both sides with honey mustard. Spread the tuna over one side of each bagel and top with bell pepper, onion, and lettuce. Place the other half of the bagel on top, cut in half, and serve with chips.

Note

If you don't have honey mustard, you can make your own by combining 2 tablespoons honey, 1 tablespoon whole-grain mustard, and 1 tablespoon Dijon mustard.

Deli Pinwheels

Each wrap makes 8 to 10 pinwheels

In the *heimish* kosher home, many of us grew up on deli roll, a Shabbat staple made from puff pastry layered with assorted deli meats and duck sauce, rolled up jelly-roll-style. It was baked until puffed and golden and then sliced. That thing was a heart attack on a plate, but oh. so. delicious. In my house, I serve a healthier version of deli pinwheels made with assorted fresh wraps that can be assembled on Shabbat. These are my favorite combinations, but feel free to experiment with wraps and fillings of your choice.

REUBEN PINWHEELS
with Russian Dressing

¼ cup mayonnaise
1 tablespoon ketchup
1 tablespoon pickle relish
1 teaspoon Frank's RedHot sauce
1 teaspoon minced onion flakes
½ teaspoon sweet paprika
1 teaspoon freshly squeezed lemon juice
Kosher salt and freshly ground black pepper to taste
3 (10-inch) whole-wheat wraps
12 slices corned beef (½ pound)
½ cup sauerkraut, squeezed dry

1.   In a small bowl, stir together the mayonnaise, ketchup, pickle relish, hot sauce, onion flakes, paprika, lemon juice, salt, and pepper.

2.   Working with one wrap at a time, spread some Russian dressing over a wrap, leaving a 1-inch border. Layer 4 slices of the corned beef along the center of the wrap and top with the sauerkraut. Roll the wrap up tightly and cut on the bias into ¾-inch-thick slices (you can nosh on the ends!). Repeat with the remaining ingredients.

ROAST BEEF
with Horseradish Aioli

½ cup mayonnaise
2 tablespoons horseradish
2 teaspoons freshly squeezed lemon juice
1 teaspoon Dijon mustard
Kosher salt and freshly ground black pepper to taste
3 (10-inch) sundried tomato wraps
9 slices roast beef (¾ pound)
1½ cups arugula

1.   In a small bowl, stir together the mayonnaise, horseradish, lemon juice, mustard, salt, and pepper.

2.   Working with one wrap at a time, spread some horseradish aioli over the wrap, leaving a 1-inch border. Layer 3 slices of the roast beef along the center of the wrap and top with ½ cup of the arugula. Roll the wrap up tightly and cut on the bias into ¾-inch-thick slices (you can nosh on the ends!). Repeat with the remaining ingredients.

DELI ROLL
with Apricot Mustard

¼ cup apricot jam

¼ cup deli mustard

3 (10-inch) plain wraps or large (flour) tortillas

8 slices smoked turkey (½ pound)

8 slices pastrami (½ pound)

1. In a small bowl, stir together the apricot jam and deli mustard.

2. Working with one wrap at a time, spread the apricot mustard over each wrap, leaving a 1-inch border. Layer 3 slices of the smoked turkey along the center of the wrap and top with 3 slices of the pastrami. Roll the wrap up tightly and cut on the bias into ¾-inch-thick slices (you can nosh on the ends!). Repeat with the remaining ingredients.

Variation
You can also serve these as wraps instead of pinwheels.

Easy Does It!
Buy store-bought dressing instead of making your own.

Arayes, Three Ways

After hasselback salami (see page 65), arayes (Middle Eastern stuffed meat pitas) take the win for my most viral recipe of all time. When I made them and posted them on my Instagram stories, the local pita factories sold out of pita (true story)! Hundreds of photos of finicky eaters who couldn't get enough poured into my DMs, and they became a household staple in homes around the world. I could think of no other way to honor this treasured dish than to make them *three* ways: the original version based on meatloaf that went viral, of course; a gluten-free "tacorayes"; and a Passover-friendly version inspired by the meat patties of my childhood. Please note, to reduce the risk of undercooked meat, I recommend using a meat thermometer to ensure that it's cooked through.

"MEATLOAF" ARAYES
Makes 16 arayes, serving 8 to 12

2 pounds ground beef (not lean)
2 extra-large egg yolks
⅓ cup ketchup
1 small Spanish onion, finely diced
2 teaspoons dried parsley
½ teaspoon garlic powder
1½ teaspoons kosher salt
1 teaspoon freshly ground black pepper
8 pitas, halved
Extra-virgin olive oil, for brushing

1. Place a baking sheet into the oven, then preheat the oven to 400°F.

2. In a large bowl, mix together the beef, egg yolks, ketchup, onion, dried parsley, garlic powder, salt, and pepper with your hands. Fill each pita pocket with ⅓ cup or more of the beef mixture (depending on the size of your pita; it should be generously packed), flattening the filling so that the pita can stand upright with the opening facing down. Brush the outside of the pitas with olive oil on both sides.

3. Remove the baking sheet from the oven and stand the pitas on the baking sheet. Bake for 5 minutes, until the meat is browned and crisp. Flip the pita onto one side and bake for 5 more minutes, until it starts to brown. Flip the pita onto the other side and bake for an additional 5 minutes, or until very crispy and toasted around the edges. Alternatively, you can grill the pita using the same method directly on grill grates or over medium-high heat on a stovetop grill pan.

Note
You can insert an instant-read thermometer into one—it should register 160°F when cooked through.

RECIPE CONTINUES

GLUTEN-FREE TACORAYES

Makes 14 arayes, serving 6 to 8

2 pounds ground beef (not lean)

½ cup pimiento-stuffed olives, diced small

3 garlic cloves, minced

1 tablespoon ground cumin

2 teaspoons smoked paprika

1 teaspoon chili powder

1 teaspoon dried oregano

1 teaspoon kosher salt

½ teaspoon freshly ground black pepper

14 (6-inch) corn tortillas

2 tablespoons canola oil, plus more
   as needed

1. In a large bowl, mix the beef, olives, garlic, cumin, paprika, chili powder, oregano, salt, and pepper. Heat the tortillas in the microwave for 30 seconds, or warm in a dry skillet to make them pliable. Spread a thick layer of the beef mixture on the left side of each tortilla, folding over the empty side to close.

2. In a large skillet over medium heat, heat 2 tablespoons canola oil. Add 2 or 3 tacorayes at a time and fry for approximately 5 minutes per side, or until the tortillas are crispy, browned, and the meat is cooked through.

Note

If the tortillas fry too quickly and the meat is not finished cooking, transfer the tacos to a rack set over a baking sheet and bake at 350°F for 5 to 10 minutes, until cooked through.

MATZARAYES
Makes 10 or 20 arayes, depending on matzo used

One of the things we eat during the Passover seder is the Hillel sandwich, which includes lettuce, horseradish, and charoset sandwiched between two pieces of matzo. After a lengthy seder, it's the last thing we eat before the festive holiday meal, so everyone is starving by then, making it especially delicious! The sandwich inspired this Passover-friendly version of arayes, which I created using the meat patty recipe that my mom makes on Passover. Feel free to use the recipe to fry up beef patties or make matzorayes—just as messy as the Hillel sandwich, only better!

1 russet potato, peeled and roughly chopped
1 carrot, peeled and roughly chopped
2 pounds ground beef (not lean)
1 small Spanish onion, grated
2 extra-large eggs
2 teaspoons kosher salt
1 teaspoon freshly ground black pepper
10 square matzos or 5 round matzos
Extra-virgin olive oil, for greasing

1. Preheat the oven to 400ºF. Place a wire cooling rack on a rimmed baking sheet and set aside.

2. In a 3-quart saucepan, cover the chopped potato and carrot with salted water then bring them to a boil over high heat. Reduce to a simmer and cook for 15 minutes, or until tender. Drain the carrots and potatoes, transfer to a large bowl, and use a potato masher to mash, set aside to cool. Add the ground beef, onion, eggs, salt, and pepper and use your hands to combine.

3. If you are using square matzo, use your hands to crack it in half. If you are using round matzo, break it into quarters. Spread ½ cup of the meat mixture onto each matzo piece (use about $1/3$ for the smaller pieces from the round matzo) and top with a second piece, like a sandwich. Brush the top and bottom pieces of matzo lightly with olive oil and transfer to the prepared baking sheet. Bake for 8 minutes, until the matzo is lightly toasted. Then flip the matzos and bake for another 8 minutes, until the matzo is toasted and the meat is cooked through. Remove from the oven and serve immediately.

Note
While this meat mixture adheres to my family's Passover customs, feel free to add additional herbs, garlic, jalapeno, or spices of your choice.

Variation
Arayes can be made with ground lamb, turkey, chicken, veal, or even fish! Try mixing ground dark meat turkey with sautéed onions and shawarma spice, or go classic with lamb, parsley, onion, cumin, coriander, and cinnamon.

Elote Schnitzel Subs

Makes 6 subs

I have probably tried every schnitzel breading that you can imagine. From panko to bread crumbs, Bissli to bagel chips, and soup croutons to falafel mix—if you can dream it, I have done it. But this stroke of genius I am especially proud of because it's just *that* good. It's inspired by *elote*, or Mexican street corn, that is grilled, slathered in chili-spiced mayonnaise, rolled in Cotija cheese, and finished with a squeeze of fresh lime juice. This crunchy schnitzel is coated in crispy corn nuts, making it perfect for oven-frying, so you can skip the mess! It's slathered in the best chili lime spread—which you're going to want to use for *everything*, from fish to fries to veggie dip.

SUB SANDWICH

6 chicken breasts (about 2 pounds)

2 (8-ounce) packages roasted, salted corn nuts (about 2⅔ cups)

1 cup all-purpose flour

Pinch of cayenne pepper

Kosher salt and freshly ground black pepper to taste

4 extra-large eggs

Juice of 1 lime

Tajín or chili-lime seasoning, for sprinkling (optional)

6 sesame baguettes or rolls, cut through the middle, toasted, if desired

Iceberg lettuce, sliced tomato, and sliced avocado, for serving

CHILI-LIME DIP

1 cup mayonnaise

Zest of 1 lime plus 1 tablespoon freshly squeezed lime juice

1 teaspoon chili powder

2 garlic cloves, minced

¼ teaspoon kosher salt

1. Preheat the oven to 400°F. Line two baking sheets with parchment paper and spray with cooking spray.

2. To prepare the chicken: Place the chicken on a piece of parchment paper and press down with the palm of your hand while you use your other hand to cut through the thickness of the breast with a knife to split it into 2 thin pieces. Repeat with the remaining chicken.

3. In the bowl of a food processor fitted with the S blade, blend the corn nuts until finely ground, then transfer them to a plate. In a shallow bowl, use a fork to combine the flour, cayenne, salt, and pepper. In a second shallow bowl, whisk together the eggs and lime juice.

4. Dip the chicken breast into the flour so both sides are well coated and shake off any excess. Next, dip the chicken into the beaten eggs, remove, and let any excess drip back into the bowl. Then dip the chicken into the ground corn nuts, pressing down to coat fully on both sides. Place the chicken on a prepared baking sheet. Repeat the breading process with the remaining chicken.

5. Bake the chicken for 15 to 20 minutes, depending on thickness, until it is opaque on the inside and cooked through. Transfer the chicken from the pan to a rack to cool (if you skip this step, the breading may turn soggy) and sprinkle with Tajín, if using.

6. To make the chili-lime dip while the chicken bakes: In a small bowl, stir together the mayonnaise, lime zest and juice, chili powder, and garlic until combined.

7. To assemble the subs, spread some chili-lime dip over both sides of the baguettes. Top with 2 pieces of schnitzel and some lettuce, tomato, and avocado. Serve immediately.

Note

Corn nuts are roasted or fried corn kernels that are sold in the snack section in major supermarkets.

Variation

You can also cut the chicken into strips and prepare these as an appetizer with the Chili-Lime Dip on the side for dunking.

Steak Tacos with Pineapple Salsa and Chimichurri

Makes 10 tacos

Taco Tuesday never looked so good!

STEAK

2 pounds skirt steak

¼ cup grapeseed oil

2 tablespoons freshly squeezed lime juice

2 garlic cloves, minced

1 teaspoon chili powder

1 teaspoon ground cumin

2 teaspoons smoked paprika

½ teaspoon dried oregano

1 teaspoon kosher salt

½ teaspoon freshly ground black pepper

ROASTED PINEAPPLE SALSA

½ ripe pineapple, cored and sliced ½ inch thick

1½ tablespoons grapeseed oil, divided

¼ teaspoon chili powder

1 small red onion, finely diced (⅓ cup)

½ red bell pepper, finely diced (⅓ cup)

1 jalapeño, seeded, veined, and finely diced

2 teaspoons freshly squeezed lime juice

1 tablespoon chopped cilantro

Kosher salt and freshly ground black pepper

Soft corn tortillas, for serving

Chimichurri (page 301), Pomegranate Pickled Onions (page 292) or Candied Jalapeños (page 292), sliced avocado (optional), and lime wedges, for serving

1. For the steak: In a baking dish, cover the skirt steak with cold water so it's fully submerged. Soak for 30 minutes at room temperature to draw out some of the salt. (Since kosher meat is salted to remove the blood [see page 14], the thin skirt steak cut is best soaked to remove some of the saltiness.) Discard the water and pat the steak dry with paper towels.

2. To a gallon-size zip-top bag, add the grapeseed oil, lime juice, garlic, chili powder, cumin, smoked paprika, oregano, salt, and pepper.

Seal and shake to mix. Add the skirt steak and marinate in the fridge for 2 hours or overnight.

3. Adjust the top oven rack to the highest position and preheat the oven to high broil.

4. Remove the skirt steak from the marinade (discard the marinade) and place it on a baking sheet. Broil the skirt steak for 5 minutes, drain the juices from the pan, turn the steak over, and broil for an additional 5 minutes. Remove the baking sheet from the oven and transfer the steak to a cutting board to rest for 10 minutes. (You may also cook the steak over high heat on a grill for 3 to 5 minutes per side.) Leave the oven on broil.

5. Drain the juices from the baking sheet and add the pineapple to it. Brush with 1 tablespoon of the grapeseed oil and sprinkle with the chili powder. Broil until the pineapple is charred around the edges, 5 minutes per side, and set aside to cool.

6. Cut the steak into 3- to 4-inch pieces, then slice each piece against the grain ¼ inch thick. Set aside and set aside to cool.

7. To make the roasted pineapple salsa: Finely dice the pineapple and place it in a medium bowl. Add the remaining ½ tablespoon grapeseed oil, the red onion, bell pepper, jalapeño, lime juice, cilantro, salt, and pepper. Stir to combine.

8. To serve, char the tortillas for a few seconds per side over an open flame on the stovetop (if you have an electric stove, you can put them in a dry pan over high heat). Serve the tortillas with the skirt steak, salsa, chimichurri, pickled onions or candied jalapeños, sliced avocado (if desired), and lime wedges.

Note

You can also make the tacos using London broil. Adjust the cooking time as needed, until medium rare.

Salads

Roasted Beet and Citrus Salad

Serves 6 to 8

People eat with their eyes first, they say, and I love to serve food that is as beautiful as it is delicious. This salad is a good example of that. A feast for the eyes and the mouth.

SALAD

2 medium red beets

1 medium golden beet

2 pink grapefruits

1 navel orange

1 small fennel bulb, cored and thinly sliced on a
  mandoline, fronds reserved for garnish

5 ounces mixed baby greens

1 small Chioggia beet, thinly sliced on a
  mandoline (optional)

CITRUS SHALLOT DRESSING

½ cup grapeseed oil

2 tablespoons freshly squeezed orange juice

3 tablespoons white wine vinegar

2 tablespoons honey

2 tablespoons minced shallot

Kosher salt and freshly ground black pepper
  to taste

1. Preheat the oven to 400°F.

2. Roast the beets: Wash the red and golden beets well, then wrap each beet individually in foil. Place the foil-wrapped beets on a baking sheet and bake for 45 minutes, or until tender when pierced with a fork. Remove the beets from the oven and cool completely before unwrapping. Once the beets have cooled, open the foil packets and pull off the skin (it should slide right off). Slice the beets ¼ inch thick.

3. Cut off the ends of the grapefruits and oranges to expose the flesh and slice off the peel following the curve of the citrus from top to bottom. Slice crosswise into ¼-inch-thick slices.

4. On a large platter, layer the beets, citrus, and fennel with the baby greens. Garnish with the raw chioggia beet slices and fennel fronds.

5. To make the dressing: In the bowl of a food processor fitted with the S blade, blend the grapeseed oil, orange juice, vinegar, honey, shallot, salt, and pepper until creamy.

6. Drizzle the dressing over the salad before serving.

Easy Does It!

Use store-bought vacuum-packed cooked beets.

Variation

To create individual stacks, layer the beet and orange slices, alternating each one so you have two of each layer. Top with a handful of greens. Drizzle with Citrus Shallot Dressing. For dairy meals, add feta. You can also sprinkle pomegranate seeds, roasted pistachios, or dukkah (page 292) over the top.

Broccoli Salad 2.0

Serves 8

Remember the broccoli salad we all grew up on? You know, the one you would find at almost every potluck—with Craisins, cashews, and ½ cup of sugar in the mayo dressing?! Yeah, that one! I don't know where the recipe came from, but it was always finished to the last drop, probably on account of all that sugar. Well, I've reimagined it just a wee bit healthier, edgier, and dare I say infinitely more delicious!

TAHINI DRESSING
½ cup tahini paste
3 tablespoons freshly squeezed lime juice
2 tablespoons honey
1 teaspoon curry powder
1 teaspoon freshly grated ginger using a rasp-style grater
1 teaspoon kosher salt
½ teaspoon red pepper flakes
¼ cup ice water

SALAD
1½ pounds broccoli, cut into bite-size pieces, including stems (peel and trim)
1 small red onion, diced
1 cup roasted, salted cashews
½ cup golden raisins

1. To make the dressing: In a small bowl, whisk together the tahini paste, lime juice, honey, curry powder, ginger, salt, red pepper flakes, and ice water.

2. To make the salad: In a large bowl, combine the broccoli, red onion, cashews, and raisins and toss with the dressing until well coated. Serve immediately.

New Age Waldorf Salad
Serves 6 to 8

If you ask me what my favorite kitchen tool is, I would probably say the julienne peeler, and this recipe showcases it well! A julienne peeler looks just like your average Y peeler, except instead of the blade having a smooth edge, it has a bunch of microblades so that when you peel, you get julienned strips. You'll never find me buying a bag of carrot matchsticks because I julienne them in a pinch, and I've put my spiralizer into storage because this peeler makes zoodling a breeze. You'll need a julienne peeler to get the perfect texture for this salad (don't try shredding the zucchini or you'll have a soggy mess!).

CANDIED WALNUTS

4 ounces raw walnut halves, chopped
1 tablespoon extra-virgin olive oil
1 tablespoon honey
½ teaspoon kosher salt

POPPY SEED DRESSING

½ cup mayonnaise
2 tablespoons apple cider vinegar
2 tablespoons honey
1 tablespoon freshly squeezed lemon juice
2 teaspoons poppy seeds

SALAD

1 zucchini (about 1 pound), julienned
1 yellow squash (about 1 pound), julienned
2 celery ribs, thinly sliced, plus 3 tablespoons celery leaves
1 large carrot, peeled and julienned
1 green apple, halved, cored, and julienned

1. To prepare the candied walnuts: Preheat the oven to 350°F. Spread the nuts on a parchment-lined baking sheet and toss with the oil, honey, and salt. Bake for 10 minutes, stirring halfway through, until the nuts are toasted and browned. Remove from the oven and set aside to cool completely.

2. To make the dressing: In a small bowl, whisk together the mayonnaise, vinegar, honey, lemon juice, and poppy seeds until creamy.

3. To make the salad: In a large serving bowl, toss the zucchini, squash, sliced celery, carrot, and apple with the dressing until coated. Top with the candied walnuts and celery leaves. Serve immediately.

Easy Does It!
Purchase store-bought candied walnuts.

Cruciferous Crunch Salad with Pomegranate Dressing

Serves 6

I'm a texture gal. Gimme all the crunch! The mouthfeel of this salad is just pure #goalzzzz. I can eat bowl after bowl and never get sick of it.

SALAD

4 cups thinly sliced curly kale

2 cups shredded red cabbage

1 kohlrabi, peeled, ends trimmed, julienned

3 radishes, thinly sliced

1 jalapeño, stem removed, thinly sliced crosswise (optional)

1 cup frozen edamame, thawed

2 whole scallions, trimmed and chopped

½ cup pomegranate seeds

⅓ cup roasted and salted sunflower seeds

POMEGRANATE DRESSING

½ cup grapeseed oil

3 tablespoons red wine vinegar

1 tablespoon pomegranate molasses

1 teaspoon soy sauce

2 tablespoons whole-grain mustard

2 tablespoons maple syrup

Kosher salt

1. To prepare the salad: In a large serving bowl, toss together the kale and cabbage. Top with the kohlrabi, radishes, jalapeño (if using), edamame, scallions, pomegranate seeds, and sunflower seeds.

2. To make the pomegranate dressing: In a small bowl, whisk together the grapeseed oil, vinegar, pomegranate molasses, soy sauce, mustard, maple syrup, and salt until creamy.

3. When ready to serve, toss the salad with the dressing.

Arugula and Delicata Squash Salad with Feta

Serves 6

Arugula is the leafy green that taught me just how much my palate has evolved. (Well, that and cilantro!) I remember when it tasted like bitter grass to me, and now I just want to eat it by the handful straight out of the bag! Its peppery bite pairs wonderfully with salty feta and sweet balsamic, and the dukkah (an Egyptian nut and spice blend) takes it over the top.

SALAD

1 medium delicata squash, sliced into ¼-inch slices, seeds removed

2 tablespoons extra-virgin olive oil

2 tablespoons honey

Kosher salt and freshly ground black pepper to taste

8 ounces arugula

4 pitted medjool dates or dried figs, halved and sliced into strips

½ small red onion, thinly sliced into half-moons

1 cup crumbled feta cheese

3 tablespoons Pistachio Dukkah (page 292)

BALSAMIC-APRICOT DRESSING

⅓ cup grapeseed oil or light olive oil

2 tablespoons balsamic vinegar

2 tablespoons apricot jam

3 tablespoons freshly squeezed orange juice

½ teaspoon kosher salt

¼ teaspoon freshly ground black pepper

1. Preheat the oven to 425°F. Place the squash on a parchment-lined baking sheet and mix with the olive oil, honey, salt, and pepper. Spread it out in an even layer. Bake for 20 to 25 minutes, until tender and starting to brown. Remove from the oven and set aside.

2. To make the dressing: In a small bowl, whisk together the grapeseed oil, vinegar, jam, orange juice, salt, and pepper until creamy.

3. To make the salad: Spread the arugula on a platter. Top with the roasted delicata squash, dates, onion, and feta. Sprinkle with the Pistachio Dukkah, drizzle with the dressing, and serve.

Easy Does It!

Use your favorite blend of seeds and roasted nuts in place of the dukkah.

Variation

Try other varieties of squash such as acorn, butternut, or kabocha, or use sweet potatoes in place of the squash.

Summer Slaw

Serves 6 to 8

Let me tell you, BBQ sauce in a salad dressing is a REV-E-LA-TION. And you'll love that this dressing is mayo-free, so it's safe to sit out on a picnic table at your next summer cookout! It's especially great with grilled chicken or fish.

SALAD

2 ears corn, husked

¼ cup grapeseed oil

Kosher salt and freshly ground black pepper
    to taste

2 ripe but firm peaches, pitted and sliced

½ large green cabbage, thinly sliced

1½ cups diagonally sliced sugar snap peas

⅓ cup Candied Jalapeños (page 292) or
    Pomegranate Pickled Onions (page 292)

BBQ DRESSING

⅓ cup grapeseed oil or light olive oil

3 tablespoons freshly squeezed lime juice

2 tablespoons barbecue sauce

1 tablespoon honey

1 teaspoon Dijon mustard

Pinch of ground cayenne pepper

Kosher salt and freshly ground black pepper
    to taste

1. Preheat a grill or grill pan to medium-high heat. Brush the corn with oil, season with salt and pepper, and grill for 10 to 12 minutes, rotating the corn until it's blackened on all sides. Slice the kernels off the cob and discard the cobs.

2. Brush the peach slices with oil and grill for 2 to 3 minutes per side, until lightly charred.

3. To make the dressing: In a small bowl, whisk together the grapeseed oil, lime juice, barbecue sauce, honey, mustard, cayenne, salt, and pepper until creamy.

4. To make the salad: In a large bowl, place the corn, peaches, cabbage, sugar snap peas, and jalapeños or onions and toss with the dressing. Serve immediately.

Easy Does It!

Use canned or frozen corn instead of fresh. Dice the peaches instead of grilling them.

Variation

If peaches aren't in season, use mango instead.

Sabich Salad

Serves 6 to 8

Sabich is the signature Iraqi pita sandwich that was traditionally eaten on Shabbat mornings, but is now a staple of Israeli street food alongside falafel. I love to serve it family-style for Shabbat lunch or for Shalosh Seudot, the third meal of Shabbat, when everyone is still full from their cholent and a light salad makes for the perfect meal.

1 medium eggplant, ends trimmed, cut into ½- to 1-inch cubes

3 tablespoons extra-virgin olive oil

Kosher salt to taste

10 ounces red cabbage (½ small head), shredded

2 tablespoons grapeseed oil

Juice of ½ lemon

3 Jammy Soft-Boiled Eggs (page 293) halved

2 plum tomatoes, sliced, or 1 bunch cherry tomatoes on the vine

2 Persian cucumbers, sliced

6 Israeli pickles, sliced in half lengthwise

3 ounces pita chips (use store-bought or bake your own, see page 62)

¾ cup Extra-Creamy Tahini (page 301)

2 tablespoons amba (mango relish)

Fresh cilantro, roughly chopped

1. Preheat the oven to 425°F. Line a baking sheet with parchment paper.

2. Place the cubed eggplant on the baking sheet, drizzle it with olive oil, and quickly toss to coat. Season with salt. Roast for 25 to 30 minutes, until fork-tender and starting to brown, tossing halfway through.

3. Meanwhile, marinate the cabbage. In a large bowl, toss the red cabbage, grapeseed oil, lemon juice, and salt together to fully coat the cabbage. Set aside while you prepare the other ingredients.

4. In the center of an oval platter, place the cabbage salad in a mound. Place the roasted eggplant, soft-boiled eggs, tomatoes, cucumbers, pickles, and pita chips around the cabbage. Drizzle with the Extra-Creamy Tahini, dollops of amba, and sprinkle with cilantro.

Loaded Eggplant Carpaccio
Serves 6 to 8

When I was growing up, my mom would often make babaganoush for Shabbat, roasting the eggplant directly on the stovetop grates for that smoky flavor. My job was to scoop the eggplant flesh out of the skin, remove the seeds, and mix it with mayonnaise, garlic, lemon, and salt to make our Ashkenazi version of the classic. This popular modern adaptation is served carpaccio-style, topped with good-quality olive oil, tahini, and various spices and toppings. I like to load it up with spices, nuts, and seeds for a full-on party in your mouth!

2 large eggplants
2 tablespoons grapeseed oil
Juice of 1 lemon
Kosher salt to taste
¼ cup Extra-Creamy Tahini (page 301)
2 tablespoons silan (date honey)
2 tablespoons extra-virgin olive oil
1 teaspoon za'atar
¼ cup pomegranate seeds
3 pitted medjool dates, chopped
2 tablespoons roasted, salted pistachios, chopped, or Pistachio Dukkah (page 292)
Fresh parsley, roughly chopped

1. With the oven rack in the highest position, preheat the broiler to high.

2. Cut the eggplants in half lengthwise and place flesh-side down on a greased baking sheet. Brush the skin with oil. Broil the eggplant for 20 to 25 minutes, until the skin is charred and the flesh is soft. Cool slightly and use a spoon to scoop out the flesh. Transfer to a serving dish (discard the skin).

3. Spread the roasted eggplant out on the dish and use a fork to lightly mash it. Season the eggplant with lemon juice and salt and gently stir to incorporate. Drizzle with Extra-Creamy Tahini, silan, and olive oil. Sprinkle with za'atar and top with pomegranate seeds, dates, pistachios, and parsley.

Variation

Top the eggplant with seasonal toppings like roasted butternut squash, beets, crumbled feta, pomegranate molasses, grated tomato, sliced jalapeño, your favorite herbs, toasted seeds, or spices like sumac and Aleppo pepper.

Passover Panzanella with Matzo Brei Croutons

Serves 6 to 8

It was the last day of Passover, and I needed to prepare yet another meal, but I was tired of cooking. I had some leftover steak in the fridge, a jar of horseradish from the seder plate that no one was ever going to eat, too much matzo, and plenty of homemade mayo. I took whatever veggies I could find and voilà—a filling and delicious salad! After an eight-day food fest, this salad was everything we wanted, and we scraped the bowl clean!

MATZO BREI CROUTONS

1 extra-large egg white, beaten
2 tablespoons extra-virgin olive oil
1 teaspoon kosher salt
¼ teaspoon dried oregano
¼ teaspoon garlic powder
¼ teaspoon freshly ground black pepper
3 square unsalted matzos or 2 round matzos

STEAK AND SALAD

1 pound London broil (preferably the shoulder blade cut)
2 tablespoons grapeseed oil
Kosher salt and butcher grind (coarse) black pepper to taste
2 heads romaine, roughly chopped
2 Persian cucumbers, thinly sliced on the diagonal
1 carrot, peeled into ribbons
4 radishes, thinly sliced
1 avocado, sliced
½ small red onion, thinly sliced

HORSERADISH DRESSING

½ cup mayonnaise
3 tablespoons grated horseradish
1 tablespoon freshly squeezed lemon juice
1 garlic clove, minced
Kosher salt and freshly ground black pepper to taste

1. To prepare the croutons: Preheat the oven to 400°F and line a baking sheet with parchment paper. In a medium bowl, whisk the egg white with the olive oil, salt, oregano, garlic powder, and pepper. Break the matzo into small pieces, about ½ inch, and add them to the bowl. Gently toss the mixture with a spoon until the matzo is fully coated, then spread it out on the baking sheet. Bake for 10 to 15 minutes, until the matzo crisps up into clusters. Remove from the oven and set aside to cool completely.

2. To prepare the steak: Rub the London broil with the grapeseed oil and season liberally with salt and pepper. (I like to use a lot of pepper so that it's pepper-crusted.) Grill over high heat or broil on a sheet pan with the oven rack in the highest position for 6 to 8 minutes per side, until the steak is charred on the outside and cooked to medium-rare. Transfer the steak to a cutting board and set aside to rest for 10 minutes. Thinly slice crosswise and against the grain.

3. To make the dressing: In a small bowl, whisk together the mayonnaise, horseradish, lemon juice, garlic, salt, and pepper until creamy. If a thinner consistency is desired, add water to thin.

4. To make the salad: In a large bowl, combine the romaine, cucumbers, carrot, radishes, avocado, and onion. Toss with the horseradish dressing. Top with the meat and the croutons and serve.

Easy Does It!

Instead of making the Matzo Brei croutons, you can toast the matzo in the oven for a few minutes to make it extra crispy, then break it apart into bite-size pieces.

Soups

Golden Milk Pumpkin Soup

Serves 6 to 8

This pumpkin soup was inspired by a winter favorite, golden milk, also called turmeric tea, an anti-inflammatory drink that I often prepare when I'm under the weather. Made with turmeric, black pepper, coconut milk, cinnamon, fresh ginger, and honey, the drink is a healthy and nutritious immune-booster that's a must-have for flu season. With its sweet and spicy flavor and creamy texture, it's as delicious as it is good for you!

1 (3-pound) butternut squash

2 tablespoons refined coconut oil

1 medium Spanish onion, diced

3 garlic cloves, minced

2-inch piece fresh ginger, peeled and minced (about 1 heaping tablespoon)

1 teaspoon ground cinnamon

1 teaspoon ground turmeric

Kosher salt and freshly ground black pepper to taste

1 cup canned full-fat coconut milk, plus more for serving

2 tablespoons honey, preferably raw for optimum health benefits

1. Preheat the oven to 400°F. Line a baking sheet with parchment paper.

2. Place the whole butternut squash on the prepared baking sheet and roast for 1 hour until fork-tender and caramelized in spots, flipping it halfway through cooking. Set aside to cool.

3. In a 6-quart pot over low heat, heat the coconut oil. Add the onion, garlic, and ginger and sweat for 10 to 15 minutes, stirring frequently, until softened but not browned. In the meantime, cut the butternut squash in half, scoop out the seeds with a spoon, and discard the seeds. Then scoop out the flesh and discard the peels.

4. Add the cinnamon and turmeric to the pot and sauté for 2 minutes, or until fragrant. Add the roasted squash, 5 cups water, salt, and pepper. Bring the soup to a boil over medium heat, then reduce to low and simmer for 20 minutes.

5. Blend the soup with an immersion blender or in a stand blender until smooth and creamy. Stir in the coconut milk and honey (for optimum health benefits, do not rewarm after adding the raw honey).

6. Divide the soup among the serving bowls and drizzle with additional coconut milk and a few cracks of pepper.

Freezer-Friendly
Store leftover soup in an airtight container in the freezer for up to 2 months.

Miso Matzo Ball Soup

Serves 6

This is the soup recipe you need for those hectic Friday afternoons when you get home late from work and need to throw together Shabbat dinner in a pinch. Or for rainy days when you need a bowl of comfort food, but you don't want to spend too much time in the kitchen. The matzo balls were inspired by scallion pancakes, and in case you were wondering, they are definitely floaters and extra fluffy at that!

SCALLION MATZO BALLS

2 extra-large eggs

1 tablespoon canola oil

1 tablespoon toasted sesame oil

½ cup matzo meal

2 scallions (green parts only), chopped

1 teaspoon baking powder

½ teaspoon kosher salt

¼ teaspoon freshly ground black pepper

SOUP

3 strips kombu (see Note), each about
    5 inches long

⅓ cup white (shiro) miso paste

Toasted nori seaweed, for serving (optional)

1. To prepare the matzo balls: In a small bowl, whisk together the eggs, canola oil, and sesame oil until well combined. Add the matzo meal, scallions, baking powder, salt, and pepper and stir with a spoon to combine. Refrigerate for 20 minutes.

2. To prepare the soup: Into a 6-quart pot, pour 8 cups of cold water and the kombu and bring to a gentle simmer over medium heat. Remove and discard the kombu. In a small bowl, place the miso, add a few ladles of the hot kombu broth, and whisk until the miso is dissolved. Pour the miso mixture back into the pot, stirring to incorporate.

3. Bring the miso broth to a simmer over medium heat. With wet hands, roll the matzo ball mixture into tablespoon-size balls and carefully add them to the soup. Gently simmer, uncovered, for 20 minutes, until the matzo balls are fluffy, turning the matzo balls over halfway through cooking.

4. Ladle the soup into bowls and serve with toasted nori, if desired.

Easy Does It!

Use store-bought matzo ball mix and prepare according to package directions, replacing 1 tablespoon of the oil with toasted sesame oil. Add the scallions and proceed as instructed.

Note

Kombu is an edible dried seaweed that can be found in health food stores or Asian grocers. It has lots of natural umami and adds a salty-savory quality to soups and stews. Eden is a popular kosher brand.

Lemony Red Lentil Soup with Saffron

Serves 6

I love a good lentil soup. Red lentils are hulled, so they cook fairly quickly—plus, they make for a super economical meal that's also nice and hearty. Add some crusty bread, and you have a perfect weeknight meal. The saffron really takes it from simple to spectacular, so don't skimp!

2 tablespoons extra-virgin olive oil

1 Spanish onion, diced small

1 carrot, peeled and diced small

2 celery stalks, diced small

3 garlic cloves, minced

½ teaspoon ground cumin

⅛ teaspoon ground cinnamon

2 dried bay leaves

1½ cups red lentils, rinsed and drained

4 cups vegetable stock

½ scant teaspoon saffron threads

Kosher salt and freshly ground black pepper to taste

½ teaspoon lemon zest

1 tablespoon freshly squeezed lemon juice

1. In a 6-quart pot over medium heat, heat the olive oil. Add the onion, carrot, celery, and garlic and sauté for 10 minutes, stirring occasionally, or until softened and starting to caramelize. Add the cumin and cinnamon and sauté for 1 minute, until fragrant. Add the bay leaves, lentils, stock, 4 cups water, the saffron, salt, and pepper. Bring the soup to a boil, reduce the heat to low, and simmer for 20 minutes, until the lentils are soft.

2. Discard the bay leaves, stir in the lemon zest and juice, and serve.

Freezer-Friendly

Store leftover soup in an airtight container in the freezer for up to 2 months.

No-Chicken Tortilla Soup

Serves 8 to 10

Chicken tortilla soup has long been a family favorite, so I set out to create a vegan version for Meatless Mondays (see page 24 for my weekly schedule). To replace pulled chicken, I use spaghetti squash for that pulled textural component, and for the protein, I add black beans. The flavor of the soup is reminiscent of tacos, a kid favorite around here, so it's a win-win all around. We like to top off a bowl with a dollop of sour cream.

1 (2-pound) spaghetti squash

2 tablespoons extra-virgin olive oil

1 medium onion, diced small

½ red bell pepper, diced small

½ green bell pepper, diced small

3 garlic cloves, minced

1 tablespoon ground cumin

2 teaspoons smoked paprika

1½ teaspoons chili powder

1 teaspoon garlic powder

Pinch of cayenne pepper

3 tablespoons tomato paste

8 cups vegetable stock

2 (14.5-ounce) cans fire-roasted diced tomatoes

1 (15.5-ounce) can black beans, drained and rinsed

Sliced avocado, fresh cilantro, thinly sliced red onion, lime wedges, sour cream, Candied Jalapeños (page 292), Homemade Tortilla Strips (page 294), for serving

1. Preheat the oven to 400°F. Line a baking sheet with parchment paper and spray with cooking spray.

2. Cut the spaghetti squash in half lengthwise and scoop out the seeds with a spoon. Place the cut-sides down on the prepared baking sheet and bake for 45 minutes, or until the squash is tender and can be pulled apart with a fork.

3. In a 6-quart stockpot over medium heat, heat the olive oil. Add the onion, bell peppers, and garlic and sauté for 5 minutes, or until the vegetables are soft but not browned. Add the cumin, smoked paprika, chili powder, garlic powder, and cayenne and continue to sauté for 2 minutes, or until fragrant. Add the tomato paste and sauté an additional 2 minutes, until it darkens in color. Add the stock, diced tomatoes with their juices, and the black beans. Cover the pot and bring the soup to a boil over high heat. Reduce the heat to medium and simmer for 20 minutes, until the soup is slightly thickened.

4. Use a fork to scrape and fluff the strands from the spaghetti squash halves (discard the skins). Divide the shredded squash between serving bowls and fill with the soup. Garnish with the toppings of your choice.

Variation

To make chicken tortilla soup, add 3 whole boneless, skinless chicken breasts to the soup along with the diced tomatoes and black beans and simmer for 20 minutes, until the chicken is cooked through. Remove the chicken from the pot and shred it with two forks. Return the pulled chicken to the soup and serve as above.

Freezer-Friendly

Store leftover soup in an airtight container in the freezer for up to 2 months.

Moroccan Carrot Soup
Serves 6

This soup was inspired by Moroccan carrot salad, an essential part of every Sephardic mezze spread and, ironically, my mom's very Ashkenazi Shabbat table. With garlic and cumin, the bold flavors are offset with fresh lemon and spicy harissa, making it light and fresh—and as one of the recipe testers attested, the sourdough gremolata deserves its own feature. It's that good!

SOUP

2 tablespoons extra-virgin olive oil

4 garlic cloves, minced

1 tablespoon ground cumin

3 pounds carrots (approximately 6 large), peeled, trimmed, and cut into medium chunks

6 cups vegetable stock

Kosher salt and freshly ground black pepper to taste

1 tablespoon Smoky Harissa (page 303 or store-bought)

1 tablespoon freshly squeezed lemon juice

Labneh or Greek yogurt, for serving (optional)

Schug (page 301), for serving (optional)

TOASTED SOURDOUGH GREMOLATA

2 slices stale sourdough (approximately 5 ounces), cut into 2-inch chunks

¼ cup extra-virgin olive oil

1 teaspoon whole cumin seed or ½ teaspoon ground cumin

2 garlic cloves, minced

Zest of ½ lemon

⅓ cup chopped fresh cilantro, parsley, or a mix

Kosher salt to taste

1. To make the soup: In a 6-quart pot, heat the olive oil over medium-low heat. Add the garlic and cumin and sauté for 2 minutes, or until fragrant. Add the carrots, stock, salt, and pepper and bring the soup to a simmer. Cook 20 to 25 minutes, until the carrots are tender.

2. Purée the soup with an immersion blender or in a stand blender until smooth and creamy. Add the harissa and lemon juice and stir to incorporate. Taste and adjust the seasonings if needed.

3. To prepare the gremolata: In a food processor fitted with the S blade or blender, pulse the sourdough to make coarse crumbs. In a 12-inch frying pan over medium heat, heat the olive oil. Add the sourdough crumbs and cumin and fry for 5 minutes, stirring often, or until the crumbs are deeply golden and crunchy. Remove from the heat and stir in the garlic, lemon zest, herbs, and salt.

4. To serve, divide the soup among bowls and sprinkle the gremolata over the tops of each bowl. If desired, add a dollop of labneh and Schug.

Easy Does It!
Omit the gremolata and garnish the soup with store-bought schug and croutons.

Freezer-Friendly
Store leftover soup in an airtight container in the freezer for up to 2 months.

Chestnut Latte Soup

Serves 4 (or 16 if serving in smaller demitasse portions)

This soup was inspired by my trip to Paris with my mom back in 2019. We would wake up each morning and head out for a hot cappuccino and an array of pastries you can only imagine. Chestnut cream is a delicacy that you'll find in many French pastries, they even sell toothpaste-style tubes of it at the market. So I set out to create a latte-inspired chestnut-based soup that's rich and velvety. My favorite way to drink this soup is out of a demitasse cup, cappuccino-style, for the full Parisian effect!

⅓ cup hazelnuts

2 tablespoons unsalted butter

2 medium shallots, finely diced (about 1 cup)

1 celery stalk, finely diced (about ½ cup)

Kosher salt to taste

3 (3.5-ounce) packages roasted chestnuts, roughly chopped

3 cups vegetable stock, plus more as needed

1 tablespoon instant espresso

¼ teaspoon freshly grated nutmeg, plus extra for serving

Freshly ground black pepper to taste

1 cup heavy cream, divided

1 tablespoon hazelnut liqueur, such as Frangelico (optional)

1. Preheat the oven to 350°F. Spread the hazelnuts on a parchment-lined baking sheet and toast for 12 to 15 minutes, shaking the pan midway through roasting, until darkened and fragrant. Remove from the oven and let the hazelnuts cool completely, then roughly chop them.

2. In a 4-quart pot, melt the butter over low heat. Add the shallots, celery, and a sprinkle of salt and sauté for 10 minutes, or until soft but not browned. Add the chestnuts and continue to sauté for 5 minutes more, or until the chestnuts soften. Add the stock, espresso, nutmeg, salt, and pepper and bring the soup to a simmer. Cook for 15 minutes, until the ingredients are tender.

3. While the soup is simmering, in the bowl of a stand mixer fitted with the whisk attachment or in a medium bowl if using a hand mixer, beat ½ cup of the heavy cream on high speed until stiff peaks form. Refrigerate until ready to serve.

4. Blend the soup with an immersion blender or using a stand blender until creamy. Stir in the remaining ½ cup heavy cream and the hazelnut liqueur (if using). Adjust the consistency of the soup by adding more stock if you prefer a thinner consistency.

5. Divide the soup among cups or bowls and top with the whipped cream, toasted hazelnuts, and freshly grated nutmeg.

Freezer-Friendly

Store leftover soup in an airtight container in the freezer for up to 2 months.

Corned Beef and Cabbage Ramen

Serves 8

I developed this recipe at my friend Dina's house. She hosted me for a holiday meal and had lots of leftover corned beef that she didn't know what to do with. After a quick tour of her pantry, I came up with this Irish/Asian fusion soup, and every bit of that leftover corned beef was finished to the last shred!

SOUP

3 pounds corned beef brisket (see Note)

2 teaspoons freshly grated ginger using a rasp-style grater

2 garlic cloves, grated using a rasp-style grater

3 tablespoons mirin

3 tablespoons soy sauce

1 tablespoon toasted sesame oil

1 teaspoon sriracha

Kosher salt to taste

4 (3-ounce) packages ramen noodles, spice packets discarded, prepared according to package directions

Optional toppings: Jammy Soft-Boiled Eggs (page 293) or Soy-Marinated Eggs (page 293), sliced scallions, sliced radishes, red pepper flakes or Chili Crisp (page 294)

CABBAGE

1 tablespoon grapeseed oil

1 teaspoon toasted sesame oil

1½ pounds green cabbage, cored and sliced ¼ inch thick

1 teaspoon soy sauce

1 teaspoon sugar

Kosher salt to taste

1. To make the soup: Remove the corned beef from the vacuum bag and rinse well under water. In a medium pot, place the corned beef and cover with water by 2 inches. Bring to a boil over high heat and then reduce to a simmer for 20 minutes. Remove the corned beef from the pot and discard the liquid.

2. Return the corned beef to the pot with 14 cups water. Bring the water to a boil over high heat, reduce the heat to low, and simmer, covered, for 2 hours, until the brisket is fork-tender. Remove the corned beef from the broth and set aside. Do not discard the broth; you should have about 8 cups.

3. Add the ginger, garlic, mirin, soy sauce, sesame oil, and sriracha to the broth and return to a simmer over medium heat. Season with salt and adjust the seasoning as desired.

4. To prepare the cabbage: In a wok or deep skillet over medium-high heat, heat the grapeseed oil and sesame oil. Add the cabbage and sauté for 5 minutes, stirring constantly, until wilted and softened. Add the soy sauce, sugar, and salt and stir to incorporate.

5. Slice the corned beef to the desired thickness (I prefer ¼ inch). Divide the corned beef, cabbage, and ramen noodles among the serving bowls. Add the hot broth to the bowls and garnish each, if desired, with an egg, scallions, radishes, and red pepper flakes or Chili Crisp.

Easy Does It!

Use prepared corned beef from your deli counter and replace the broth with store-bought beef stock. Use a bag of preshredded cabbage and blanch it in the broth for a few minutes to soften instead of sautéing it.

Note

Corned beef is traditionally made from beef brisket that has been brined in a pickling solution and is often sold vacuum sealed. You may substitute any cut of corned beef here, just simmer until fork-tender.

Freezer-Friendly

You may freeze the cooked corned beef and stock separately.

Deconstructed Wonton Soup

Serves 8 to 10

Wonton soup is always our soup of choice when we go out to Chinese restaurants. Half the kids only eat the wonton skins, and the others like the filling of spiced ground turkey or meat, so I came up with this deconstructed version to make everyone happy! With ground turkey, egg noodles, and a light Asian broth, it makes a full meal in a bowl.

WONTON FILLING

2 pounds ground dark meat chicken or turkey

1- to 1 ½-inch piece fresh ginger, peeled and grated using a rasp-style grater (about 1 teaspoon)

3 garlic cloves, grated using a rasp-style grater

3 scallions, thinly sliced (whites and greens divided)

2 tablespoons soy sauce

1 teaspoon toasted sesame oil

½ teaspoon sriracha

½ teaspoon kosher salt

¼ teaspoon freshly ground black pepper

SOUP

1 tablespoon grapeseed oil

1 teaspoon toasted sesame oil

12 cups chicken broth

3 tablespoons soy sauce

3 tablespoons mirin

Kosher salt to taste

12 ounces wide egg noodles, cooked according to package directions

Red pepper flakes or Chili Crisp (page 294), and scallions, for serving (optional)

1. To prepare the wonton filling: In a medium bowl, stir together the ground chicken, ginger, garlic, scallion whites, soy sauce, sesame oil, sriracha, salt, and pepper.

2. To make the soup: In a 6-quart pot over medium heat, heat the grapeseed oil and sesame oil. Add the chicken mixture and cook for 6 minutes, using a wooden spoon to break up and stir the mixture, or until the chicken is cooked through and no longer pink. Add the chicken broth, soy sauce, and mirin and bring the soup to a simmer. Season with salt.

3. Stir the cooked egg noodles into the soup and serve immediately with the reserved scallion greens and red pepper flakes (if using).

Note

If preparing in advance, wait to add the egg noodles until right before serving.

Freezer-Friendly

Store leftover soup in an airtight container (without the egg noodles) and freeze for up to 2 months.

Mushroom-Cauli Soup

Serves 8

Mushroom barley soup is a family favorite, cozy dinner reserved for cold winter nights. I developed this gluten-free version during my Paleo diet days, adding marrow bones for that unctuous quality you normally get from barley and using cauliflower rice as a carb-free stand-in. The results were so spot-on, no one even noticed the difference!

1 tablespoon extra-virgin olive oil

2 pounds boneless flanken (cross-cut short ribs)

1 pound marrow bones

Kosher salt and freshly ground black pepper to taste

1 large leek (white and pale green parts only), washed and thinly sliced

3 garlic cloves, minced

2 celery stalks, diced

2 medium parsnips, peeled and diced

10 ounces baby bella mushrooms, stemmed, thinly sliced

10 ounces oyster mushrooms, stemmed, thinly sliced

3½ ounces shiitake mushrooms, stemmed, thinly sliced

4 cups beef or chicken stock

4 sprigs of fresh thyme

1 tablespoon soy sauce

1 dried bay leaf

2 cups cauliflower rice (fresh or frozen)

1. In a large Dutch oven over medium heat, heat the olive oil. Season the flanken and marrow bones with salt and pepper and sear for 5 minutes on each side, until browned. Use tongs to transfer the meat and bones to a plate and set aside.

2. In the Dutch oven, place the leeks, garlic, celery, and parsnips and sauté for 6 to 8 minutes, stirring occasionally, until softened. Add the mushrooms and continue to sauté for 5 minutes, until the mushrooms soften. Use a wooden spoon to scrape the bits from the bottom of the pot as they cook.

3. Return the meat to the pot along with any accumulated juices, the stock, 4 cups water, the thyme, soy sauce, bay leaf, salt, and pepper. Bring the soup to a boil over high heat, reduce to low, and simmer, covered, for 1½ hours, until the meat is soft.

4. Before serving, add the cauliflower rice to the pot and simmer over medium heat for 5 minutes, until tender.

5. To serve, divide the marrow bones and meat among the bowls. Add the soup and serve with crusty bread for dipping into the marrow.

Freezer-Friendly

To freeze this soup, omit the cauliflower rice. Store in an airtight container in the freezer for up to 2 months. Add cauliflower rice before serving.

It's Tradition!

World Peace Challah
Makes 1 large pull-apart challah

When the popular website The Kitchn did one of their side-by-side recipe comparisons of the best challah recipe, I was so honored that my challah came out as the winner! The one request I have repeatedly received is to scale down the recipe to make just one or two, and it's finally here! I bake this recipe pull-apart style so that you can add different toppings to please everyone at the table. In heimish bakeries, it's sometimes referred to as Shalom Bayit Challah, which translates to "peace in the home," but I'm thinking even bigger—world peace!

1 (¼-ounce) packet active dry yeast (about 2¼ teaspoons)

1 teaspoon sugar

1 cup warm water

½ cup honey

¼ cup canola oil, plus 1 tablespoon for greasing the dough

2 extra-large eggs, divided

2 teaspoons kosher salt

4 cups bread flour, plus more for kneading

Optional toppings (approximately 1 tablespoon per section): Sweet crumbs (see Note), za'atar, nigella seeds, raw sesame seeds, Everything Bagel Spice (page 305), sea salt, poppy seeds, dried herbs, minced onion, garlic flakes

1. In a large bowl, mix the yeast, sugar, and water with a spoon, then let it rest for 5 minutes, until the yeast starts to bloom. Add the honey, ¼ cup oil, 1 of the eggs, and the salt and stir with a spoon to incorporate.

2. Add half of the flour and mix with a spoon until creamy. Add the remaining flour and knead by hand in the bowl until your dough is smooth, elastic, and no longer sticky, adding more flour if needed.

3. When you are done kneading, grease the dough with 1 tablespoon oil and cover the bowl with a clean kitchen towel. Put it in a warm place (I like to set my oven to 200°F and put the bowl on top of the oven) and leave the dough to rise for 1½ to 2 hours, until doubled in size.

4. Punch down the dough with your hands and use a knife or bench scraper to divide it into 7 equal portions. Using your hands, roll each portion of dough into a ball. Place 1 ball in the center of a 10-inch round cake pan and surround the center ball with the remaining 6 balls of dough. Let the dough rise in a warm spot, uncovered, for 30 more minutes, until the balls are touching each other.

5. Preheat the oven to 350°F. In a small bowl, beat the remaining egg. Brush the dough with the egg and sprinkle with the topping of your choice. Bake for 35 minutes, or until golden brown. Check the bottom of the challah. It should be browned and sound hollow when you tap on it.

6. Remove the challah from the pan and set it on a rack to cool. Serve within 1 or 2 days. If desired, you can warm the challah in a 350°F oven for 15 minutes before serving.

Note
To make sweet crumbs, combine 1 tablespoon all-purpose flour, 1 tablespoon sugar, 1½ teaspoons canola oil, and a pinch of salt and mix it with your fingers until crumbly.

Freezer-Friendly
To freeze the challah, wrap it in parchment paper, foil, and a zip-top bag and freeze for up to 3 months.

The Rebbetzin's Gefilte Fish

Makes 30 gefilte fish patties

For eighteen years, my father had the privilege to work as a caretaker in the home of the Lubavitcher Rebbe, Rabbi Menachem Mendel Schneerson, a world leader whose global influence and teachings continue to inspire the world over—The Rebbe was even posthumously awarded the Congressional Medal of Honor for his contributions toward peace and education. One of my father's responsibilities was preparing homemade gefilte fish, which he had learned to make from the Rebbe's wife, Rebbetzin Chaya Mushkah, or as we affectionately called her, Doda (which means "aunt" in Hebrew). This sacred family recipe is one that my parents prepared together every eve of Passover. It is simple to make, yet it carries the most special and cherished family memories. It is my honor and privilege to share it with you.

GEFILTE FISH

2 large carrots, peeled and roughly chopped
1 large Spanish onion, quartered
2 pounds ground carp
1 pound ground pike
1 pound ground whitefish*
4 extra-large eggs
½ cup sugar
1½ tablespoons kosher salt
Whitefish steaks (optional; see Notes)

BROTH

3 carrots, peeled and sliced into ¼-inch-thick coins
2 celery stalks, cut into ¼-inch-thick slices
1 Spanish onion, halved and sliced into
  half-moons
¼ cup sugar, or to taste
2 tablespoons kosher salt
2 pounds fish heads and bones, thoroughly
  cleaned (see Notes)
1 pound carp fish roe (optional)

1. To make the gefilte fish: In the bowl of a food processor fitted with the S blade, grind the carrots and onion until finely ground, scraping the bowl with a rubber spatula as needed.

2. In a large bowl, combine the ground carrots and onion, carp, pike, whitefish, eggs, sugar, and salt, mixing to incorporate. Cover the bowl and refrigerate the gefilte fish mixture while you prepare the broth.

3. To make the broth: In a 12-quart pot, place the sliced carrots, celery, and onion. Fill the pot one-quarter full with cold water, add the sugar and salt, and bring to a simmer over medium heat. Add the fish heads and bones and return to a simmer. Gently add the fish roe (if using) to the pot.

4. While the broth is simmering, remove the gefilte fish from the fridge and, using wet hands, portion it out into oval-shaped patties, about ⅓ cup each. Gently add the gefilte fish to the broth, ensuring that it is constantly simmering. Add stuffed whitefish steaks (if using, see note). Gently simmer the patties over low heat, covered, for 3 hours, until the broth is jellied and thickened, adding water as needed to keep the fish mostly covered.

5. When the gefilte fish is done cooking, remove it from the heat and let it cool completely in the broth. Remove the fish heads and bones with a slotted spoon and discard. Transfer the gefilte fish to a large shallow pan along with the vegetables and as much of the broth as desired. Cover with foil and refrigerate for up to 5 days. Serve cold with *chrein* (sweet beet horseradish relish).

Notes

This is a freshwater species called "whitefish," not a white-fleshed fish like cod or haddock. Found in America or Canada in the Great Lakes, it's what is used to make gefilte fish.

Notes, cont.

- I order the fish preground from my fishmonger along with the fish heads and bones from the fish carcasses. If you can't order preground fish, you can order skinless, boneless fillets and grind the fish in your food processor until finely ground. If you can't get heads and bones for the stock, you may omit them.

- As per my family's tradition, we do not use many processed ingredients on Passover, not even black pepper is allowed. As such, this recipe is seasoned only with salt and sugar (we always used a simple syrup that my mom prepared for the holiday), and no matzo meal was added. In the Rebbe's home, no sugar was added to the fish.

- One of the ways that my mother used to serve the gefilte fish was to stuff it into the empty cavity of whitefish steaks (see photo). If you would like to prepare a few portions that way, stuff a portion of gefilte fish into the empty cavity and seal the ends closed with a toothpick. Gently add the whitefish steaks to the broth along with the gefilte fish patties and cook as above.

- Use this recipe as a guide and adapt it to your liking. For a sweeter fish, use more whitefish and less carp. You can also reduce the sugar and add pepper, if desired.

Golden Chicken Soup

Serves 12

Is there anything better than a bowl of Jewish penicillin? It's the smell of Shabbat, the comfort food after a tummy ache, the hug of a Jewish grandma. Chicken soup is a meal in a bowl and can be adapted to your liking, so I encourage you to use this recipe merely as a guide. Add your favorite herbs, veggies, and noodles to make this chicken soup *your* chicken soup.

1 pound chicken necks, wings, and/or feet

1 turkey neck

3 peeled garlic cloves

2 dried bay leaves

½ tablespoon whole black peppercorns

3 sprigs of fresh thyme

½ bunch of fresh dill, parsley, or a mix

3 pounds chicken legs on the bone, skin removed

2 carrots, peeled and cut into 1-inch chunks

2 celery stalks, cut into 1-inch chunks

1 large leek, washed and sliced in half lengthwise

1 small Spanish onion, peel on, ends trimmed (this helps give the soup a golden color)

1 medium zucchini, cut into 1-inch coins

2 tablespoons kosher salt

Traditional matzo balls (optional; use the scallion matzo balls recipe on page 108 and replace sesame oil with canola oil and omit scallions)

Mandlach (soup croutons) or egg noodles, for serving (optional)

1. Into a soup bag or cheesecloth, place the chicken necks, turkey neck, garlic cloves, bay leaves, peppercorns, thyme, and dill. Into a second soup bag or cheesecloth, place the chicken legs. Into a 10-quart pot, place the bags and cover with cold water until almost full (about 2 inches from the top of the pot).

2. Cover the pot, leaving the lid slightly ajar, and bring to a boil over medium-high heat, removing any impurities that rise to the top with a skimmer or spoon until the broth is clear.

3. Add the carrots, celery, leek, onion, zucchini, and any other vegetables of your choice and season with salt. Continue to cook the soup, with the lid slightly ajar, over medium-low heat so that it maintains a gentle simmer. Cook for a minimum of 3 hours, until the soup is fragrant and golden, but the longer, the better!

4. When the soup is done, remove the bags of necks and herbs and discard. Take the chicken legs out of the bag, separate the meat from the bones, and tear the meat into bite-size chunks (discard the bones). Return the chicken to the soup.

5. If preparing matzo balls, you can cook the balls separately in salted boiling water or directly in the soup broth, simmering for 20 minutes, until fluffy.

6. Ladle the soup into bowls with chunks of vegetables, chicken, and matzo balls (if using). Add croutons or egg noodles, if desired.

Variation

For immune-boosting chicken soup, add a stalk of lemongrass, a 2-inch chunk of peeled fresh turmeric, and a 2-inch chunk of peeled fresh ginger to the spice bag.

Freezer-Friendly (stock only)

I do not freeze leftover chicken or vegetables; however, you can freeze leftover chicken broth in 16-ounce deli containers or ice cube trays to add flavor to rice, soups, stews, and sauces.

Ma's Perfect Potato Kugel

Serves 12

Potato kugel is pure comfort food for me. It transports me to my bubby's kitchen on Friday afternoons, where I'd be lucky enough to get a hot piece straight from the oven. (Sometimes Bubby would grate in a zucchini, and that was my favorite!) Ma's kugel is equally comforting and my all-time guilty pleasure—so much so that I don't like to have it around because I will eat it. All of it. So, I leave the potato kugel cooking to my mom, and I go over for a piece or two before Shabbat and the holidays, taking my children with me so that they, too, can cherish their own special memories of Bubby's potato kugel.

½ cup canola oil, plus ⅓ cup for greasing the pan
5 extra-large eggs, beaten
¼ cup matzo meal
2 tablespoons kosher salt
1 teaspoon coarsely ground black pepper
8 large russet potatoes, peeled and cut into 1-inch chunks
1 large Spanish onion, cut into eighths
Yellow mustard, for serving (optional)

1. In a large bowl, combine ½ cup oil, the eggs, matzo meal, salt, and pepper and whisk until combined.

2. In the bowl of a food processor fitted with the S blade, grind the potatoes and onions in batches until finely minced but not ground, combining the potatoes and onions as you add them to the machine (this keeps the potatoes from browning). Transfer the ground potato and onions to the egg mixture as you go.

3. Grease a 9 × 13-inch baking dish with the remaining ⅓ cup oil and place in the oven while it preheats to 450°F. Carefully remove the baking dish from the oven and pour the potato mixture into the pan, spreading it out evenly. Return the dish to the oven and bake for 35 to 40 minutes, until the top is browned.

4. Reduce the oven temperature to 350°F and bake for an additional 35 to 40 minutes, until the top is deeply browned and crispy.

5. Serve hot with yellow mustard (try it!). Store leftovers in the refrigerator, wrapped in foil, for up to 3 days.

Note

For years, my mom used the shredding disc instead of the S blade to grind the kugel, but when she switched over, we all loved the piecey consistency better than the stringy one. Feel free to use whichever attachment you prefer.

Cholent with Quick Kishke

Serves 12

I suffer from something I like to call "fleishphobia," a fear of being fleishigs, Yiddish for "meaty." Since kosher-keepers are required to wait 3 to 6 hours after eating meat before drinking or eating anything made with milk, some people pass on cholent, the traditional Shabbat afternoon stew that is cooked overnight (a custom that developed to conform with Jewish laws that prohibit cooking on the Sabbath) in favor of their midday coffee or chocolate fix. I am one of those people, although I do make cholent every week because it's just not Shabbat without it! And of course I always have to serve it with kishke, a log of stuffing that is a common Ashkenazi addition to cholent. Old-school kishke is stuffed into beef intestine (*kishke* is Yiddish for "intestine"), but nowadays it's made in synthetic, inedible casings. This quick vegan version uses oil instead of shmaltz and corn flake crumbs for added sweetness and texture. It comes together easily with a spoon.

CHOLENT

½ cup cholent beans (see Notes)

1 cup pearled barley

1 medium Spanish onion, diced small (sauté in oil until caramelized before using for extra flavor)

3 russet potatoes, peeled and diced into 1-inch chunks

1 pound marrow bones

1 pound flanken (cross-cut short ribs), kolichol (beef shank), or beef cheek

1 pound chunk pastrami, preferably navel (optional)

2 teaspoons smoked paprika

2 teaspoons kosher salt

1 teaspoon freshly ground black pepper

1 teaspoon ground cumin

1 teaspoon ground turmeric

1 tablespoon soy sauce

2 tablespoons ketchup

2 tablespoons honey

4 cups chicken stock

6-inch piece Ma's Perfect Potato Kugel (page 133), optional

QUICK KISHKE

1 cup all-purpose flour

½ cup store-bought corn flake crumbs

½ cup chicken stock

½ cup canola oil

1 tablespoon sugar

1 tablespoon sweet paprika

1 teaspoon garlic powder

1 teaspoon onion powder

1 teaspoon kosher salt

1 teaspoon coarsely ground black pepper

1. To make the cholent: In a 6-quart slow cooker insert, layer the beans, barley, onion, potatoes, marrow bones, flanken, pastrami, paprika, salt, pepper, cumin, and turmeric. Add the soy sauce, ketchup, and honey and pour the stock over the mixture to distribute the spices (don't stir). Add 1 cup water. The cholent should be mostly covered with liquid.

2. To prepare the kishke: In a medium bowl, stir together the flour, corn flake crumbs, chicken stock, canola oil, sugar, sweet paprika, garlic powder, onion powder, salt, and pepper. Spread the mixture onto a 17-inch piece of parchment paper, tightly shape it into a 10-inch-long log, wrap, and twist the ends tightly to seal.

3. Place the kishke on top of the cholent. Wrap the potato kugel (if using) in foil and place it on the top, as well.

4. Set the slow cooker on low right before Shabbat and cook overnight until serving. The stew will be thick and hearty. Transfer it to a serving bowl and top with sliced kishke, potato kugel, meat, and marrow bones.

Notes

• *I use a prepared dried bean mix labeled "cholent mix," but you can use kidney beans, pinto beans, or any beans you like. If you like a bean-heavy cholent, add more beans. Just make sure to add extra water so it doesn't dry out.*

• *To make a pareve cholent, omit the meat and bones. Cut a log of kishke in half. Wrap half in foil for the top of the cholent. Dice the second half into chunks and spread around the cholent.*

Tip

For easier cleanup, I like to line my slow cooker with a wide sheet of parchment paper or a slow-cooker liner.

Bubby's Stuffed Cabbage

Serves 12

It's not Simchat Torah without stuffed cabbage simmering on the stove, a recipe that was handed down from my bubby, who shared it with me one year when I was writing an editorial for Passover (I used mashed potatoes in the filling instead of rice!). Stuffed cabbage is traditionally served on Simchat Torah because the stuffed leaves are said to resemble Torah scrolls.

STUFFED CABBAGE

1 large head green cabbage

2 pounds ground beef (not lean)

¾ cup uncooked long-grain white rice

1 small Spanish onion, grated

2 tablespoons ketchup (optional)

2 extra-large eggs

Kosher salt and freshly ground black pepper to taste

TOMATO SAUCE

1 Granny Smith apple, peeled and grated

1 large tomato, cored and diced small

¼ cup golden raisins

3 (15-ounce) cans tomato sauce

½ cup sugar, or to taste

Juice of 1 lemon

Kosher salt and freshly ground black pepper to taste

1. To prepare the cabbage: Place the cabbage in the freezer overnight or for about 12 hours. Remove the cabbage from the freezer and place it in a colander in the sink to defrost. (This step makes the cabbage leaves pliable for rolling and stuffing.) The cabbage will take several hours to defrost so make sure to remove it from the freezer in advance.

2. In a large bowl, combine the ground beef, rice, onion, ketchup (if using), eggs, salt, and pepper. Place the filling in the fridge while you prepare the cabbage leaves.

3. Remove the tough outer leaves of the cabbage and set aside a few leaves to line the pot. Peel the remaining large leaves from the base, taking care not to tear the cabbage as you go. Set the whole leaves aside and chop up the remaining cabbage to reserve for the sauce.

4. With a paring knife, trim the thick part of the stem off the base of the leaves, taking care not to cut through the rest of the leaf. Place the leaves so that they are curling upward like a bowl.

5. Place ⅓ cup of the filling toward the base of each leaf and fold the leaf on each long side over the filling. Roll the cabbage leaf up tightly from the base of the leaf to the tip. Continue with the remaining leaves. If you have any leftover filling, simply divide and roll it into small meatballs and set aside to place in the pot later alongside the cabbage rolls.

6. Line an 8-quart pot with the reserved cabbage leaves. Place the stuffed cabbage rolls, seam-side down, into the pot. Add the reserved chopped cabbage, apple, tomato, and raisins to the pot with the cabbage rolls.

7. In a large measuring cup, mix the tomato sauce with the sugar, lemon juice, salt, and pepper. Pour the mixture over the cabbage rolls.

8. Bring the sauce to a gentle boil over medium heat and then reduce to a simmer. If you have any meatballs, gently add them to the simmering sauce. Partially cover the pot, leaving it slightly ajar so that the steam does not force the cabbage rolls open. Cook for approximately 2 hours, or until the cabbage is tender and the sauce has thickened.

Variation

For cabbage soup, shred the cabbage and roll the meat mixture into small balls. Into a large soup pot, place the cabbage and sauce ingredients and bring to a simmer. Add the meatballs and cook, covered, over medium heat for 2 hours, or until the soup is thick and the meatballs are tender.

Fins & Scales

Stuffed Branzino

Serves 2

Whole roasted fish is so underrated. It cooks up quickly and retains its moisture, so you get a light and flaky main in just 20 minutes. Using leftover relish, tapenade, or pesto makes a great flavor booster to branzino's blank canvas. The flavor-packed Sundried Tomato Tapenade marries so well with the fish's mild sweetness, and it can be easily doubled or tripled to serve more people.

1 (1- to 1½-pound) branzino, scaled and gutted
½ recipe Sundried Tomato Tapenade (page 300)
1 lemon, thinly sliced into rounds
2 tablespoons extra-virgin olive oil
Kosher salt and freshly ground black pepper to taste
Capers and chopped fresh parsley, for garnish
Lemon wedges, for serving

1. Preheat the oven to 450°F. Line a baking sheet with parchment paper.

2. Open the fish and spread the tapenade over the flesh. Add the lemon slices on top of the tapenade and close the fish. Transfer the fish to the prepared baking sheet. Cut three shallow slits into the flesh on the top of the fish, drizzle with olive oil, and season with salt and pepper.

3. Bake the fish for 20 minutes, until the flesh is opaque and flakes easily with a fork. Remove from the oven, transfer to a platter, garnish with capers and fresh parsley and serve with lemon wedges.

Note

You can use any 1- to 3-pound fish for this recipe such as snapper, perch, cod, arctic char, bass, or sea bream. Bake for an additional 5 to 10 minutes for a larger fish. For fish fillets, top with tapenade, drizzle with olive oil and a squeeze of lemon, and roast, uncovered, at 425°F for 15 to 20 minutes, until the fish is opaque and flakes easily with a fork.

Apple and Honey Mustard Salmon

Serves 8

When I was twelve years old, my family was gathered around the table for the pre–Yom Kippur feast, when there was a car accident on the main parkway outside our home. My older brother, Ari, who had recently earned his EMT certification, dashed outside the door to help. Every year, on the eve of Yom Kippur, we remember Ari and his bravery by eating the honey mustard salmon my mom was serving that day. This recipe was inspired by that dish and my brother Ari's loving memory. I like to serve it on Rosh Hashanah as a sort of prayer that the good should overpower the bad and that we should all merit to see the "honey" in our lives and not know of any bitter "mustard."

⅓ cup apricot jam

2 tablespoons whole-grain mustard

2 tablespoons Dijon mustard

2 tablespoons honey, plus more for drizzling

Kosher salt and freshly ground black pepper to taste

2-pound side of salmon, pin bones removed

1 red apple, cored, halved, and thinly sliced

1 green apple, cored, halved, and thinly sliced

2 tablespoons extra-virgin olive oil

Juice of ½ lemon

1. Preheat the oven to 400°F. Line a baking sheet with parchment paper.

2. In a small bowl, combine the apricot jam, whole-grain mustard, Dijon mustard, honey, salt, and pepper.

3. Place the salmon on the prepared baking sheet. Brush the mixture generously over the salmon flesh. Decorate the salmon by laying the apple slices on the flesh of the fish, alternating between red and green and overlapping slightly, until the salmon is fully covered. Drizzle the decorated salmon with the olive oil, lemon juice, and more honey.

4. Bake, uncovered, for 25 minutes, basting once with the pan juices halfway through cooking. The fish should be opaque and flake easily with a fork.

5. Serve warm or at room temperature.

Tuna Zoottanesca

Serves 2 or 3

Pasta puttanesca is a classic Italian pasta dish made with anchovies, garlic, capers, and black olives cooked in a rich tomato sauce. Even if you're put off by anchovies, be brave and give them a try. You'll find that they don't taste fishy at all; rather, they add a salty, umami flavor to the sauce and are barely even detectable. Using zoodles in place of pasta makes this a great brunch dish or light Motzash (post-Shabbat) meal that's pantry-friendly and super quick to throw together. The tuna packs in the protein, and the olive oil brings the healthy fats and bold flavor that meld together wonderfully with this humble but flavor-packed dish aptly named Zoottanesca by my food stylist, Chaya, for the zoodle + puttanesca fusion.

6 ounces good-quality tuna packed in olive oil

4 anchovy fillets

4 garlic cloves

¼ teaspoon red pepper flakes

1 (14.5-ounce) can diced tomatoes with their juices

1 (8-ounce) can tomato sauce

⅓ cup sliced black canned olives

2 tablespoons drained capers

Juice of ½ lemon

Kosher salt to taste

Pinch of sugar (optional)

1 zucchini, julienned with a julienne peeler or spiralized

Fresh parsley, roughly chopped, for garnish

1. Into a large skillet, drain the olive oil from the tuna and set the tuna aside. Heat the oil over medium heat and add the anchovies. Cook for 2 minutes, or until the anchovies dissolve into the oil. Add the garlic and red pepper flakes and continue to sauté for 1 minute, or until fragrant. Stir in the diced tomatoes, tomato sauce, olives, capers, lemon juice, and salt. Bring the mixture to a simmer and cook, covered, for 10 minutes, until saucy. Taste the sauce; if it's very acidic, add a pinch of sugar.

2. Uncover the pan and add the zucchini. Simmer for 2 minutes, until the zucchini is just tender. Add the canned tuna and cook 1 more minute, until heated through. Garnish with parsley and serve immediately.

Variation

Use ¼ pound spaghetti in place of zoodles. Cook the spaghetti until al dente and add to the sauce in place of the zoodles.

Fish in Chips!

Serves 6 to 8

To be honest, my kids are not the biggest fish eaters, and the only way I can really get them to eat fish is out of a box (frozen fish sticks for the win!) or fried with a side of french fries. So I combined the fish and the chips to make the ultimate french-fried fish sticks that my son says taste just like tater tots, thanks to a coating made from instant mashed potato flakes. And who doesn't LOVE tater tots?! I save the brine from my pickle jars exclusively to marinate the fish—but if you have to drain a jar of pickles just for the brine, use the pickles to make fried pickles (see page 46).

FRIED FISH

2 pounds white fish fillets (about 4 fillets; see Note)

1¼ cups pickle brine (from 16-ounce jar of pickles)

1 cup all-purpose flour

2 teaspoons smoked paprika, divided

2½ teaspoons kosher salt, divided

½ teaspoon freshly ground black pepper

3 extra-large eggs

1½ teaspoons yellow mustard

1½ teaspoons Frank's RedHot sauce

2 cups instant mashed potato flakes

½ teaspoon garlic powder

½ teaspoon onion powder

⅛ teaspoon cayenne pepper

Canola oil, for frying

Lemon wedges, for serving

PICKLE AIOLI

½ cup mayonnaise

1 tablespoon pickle brine

1 garlic clove, minced

2 teaspoons Dijon mustard

1 teaspoon freshly squeezed lemon juice

2 tablespoons minced pickles (optional)

Kosher salt and freshly ground black pepper to taste

1. To prepare the fish: Cut the fish fillets in half lengthwise down the center and then cut each half into 2 long strips. Cut all the strips in half crosswise so you have 8 fish sticks per fillet. In a large bowl, place the fish sticks and cover them with the pickle brine. Set the fish aside to marinate for 30 minutes at room temperature and then discard the brine.

2. To make the aioli: In a small bowl, combine the mayonnaise, pickle brine, garlic, Dijon, lemon juice, minced pickles (if using), salt, and pepper. Cover with plastic and refrigerate until serving.

3. Set up a three-bowl dredging station. In the first medium bowl, place the flour, 1 teaspoon of the paprika, 1 teaspoon of the salt, and pepper and mix well. In the second medium bowl, whisk together the eggs, yellow mustard, and hot sauce until combined. In the third medium bowl, whisk together the mashed potato flakes, remaining 1 teaspoon paprika, remaining 1½ teaspoons salt, garlic powder, onion powder, and cayenne.

4. In a large skillet over medium heat, heat ½ inch of canola oil. Test the oil by adding a pinch of flour; it should bubble as soon as it hits the oil.

5. Working in batches, coat a few of the fish strips in the flour mixture, then dip them into the eggs, allowing the excess to drip off, and then coat in the mashed potato flakes, shaking off the excess. Fry the fish in the oil for 3 to 4 minutes per side, until the breading is

golden and the fish is flaky, taking care not to overcrowd the pan and adding oil as needed. Drain the fish sticks on paper towels to absorb excess oil and transfer to a rack set over a baking sheet to keep them crispy while you fry the other batches.

6. Serve the fish sticks with lemon wedges and the pickle aioli for dipping.

Note

You may use any flaky white fish such as tilapia, cod, flounder, or Nile perch.

Pastrami-Style Gravlax

Serves 12

I've never been much of a lox person, mostly because I'm not the biggest fan of its texture. But pastrami lox changed everything: it was my gateway lox. Its smoky, spicy rub crusts the fish, giving it some texture—it was love at first bite!

PASTRAMI RUB

¼ cup ground coriander

2 tablespoons smoked paprika

1 tablespoon coarsely ground black pepper

1 tablespoon mustard seed

1 tablespoon dry mustard

1 teaspoon onion powder

1 teaspoon garlic powder

CURING RUB

1 cup kosher salt

½ cup granulated sugar

½ cup (packed) dark brown sugar

GRAVLAX

3 pounds center-cut skin-on salmon fillet, pin bones removed

⅓ cup silan (date honey)

Capers, cornichons, olives, thinly sliced radish, thinly sliced red onion, alfalfa sprouts, sliced tomatoes on the vine, cucumbers sliced on a bias, avocado, sliced lemon, bagels, crackers, or sliced baguette, for serving (optional)

1. To make the pastrami rub: In a small bowl, combine the coriander, paprika, pepper, mustard seed, dry mustard, onion powder, and garlic powder.

2. To make the curing rub: In a second small bowl, combine the salt, granulated sugar, and brown sugar.

3. To prepare the salmon: Spread half of the pastrami rub on the salmon, reserving the remaining rub in an airtight storage container for later. Cut the salmon in half crosswise.

4. Spread a third of the curing rub on a long sheet of plastic wrap and lay half of the salmon, skin-side down, on top. Spread another third of the rub on top of the salmon. Place the second piece of salmon on top of the first piece, flesh-side down. Place the remaining third of the curing rub on top of the skin of the second piece of salmon, ensuring that both pieces are fully coated on all sides. Wrap the fish tightly in two layers of plastic wrap.

5. Place the salmon on a baking sheet. Lay a cutting board on top of the fish and weigh down the board with a few heavy cans. Place the entire tray with the salmon and weights in the refrigerator for 24 hours. Remove the salmon from the fridge and drain and discard any liquid that has collected on the baking sheet (do not unwrap the salmon). Flip the salmon "package" over, top with the cutting board and weights and refrigerate for an additional 24 hours.

6. Unwrap the fish and drain off any accumulated liquid. Separate the salmon so that they are both flesh-side up. Brush off the spices and salt with a paper towel and pat the fish dry. Use a basting brush to coat the flesh of the fish with silan and pat the reserved pastrami rub over it. Return the fish to the refrigerator on a baking sheet, uncovered, for 12 hours or overnight.

7. Remove the salmon from the fridge. Use a sharp knife to slice the salmon very thinly crosswise against the grain. Discard the salmon skin.

8. Serve the gravlax on a platter with all the trimmings.

Freezer-Friendly

Store the salmon in an airtight container in the refrigerator for up to 3 days or freeze for up to 1 month.

Simply Crudo with Cilantro Crema

Serves 4

Many people turn their nose up at fish because they feel like it's too, well, *fishy*. But it really comes down to a few simple rules. Fresh fish should smell like the ocean. Its flesh should be firm and smooth, its color vibrant and not dull, and its eyes should bulge and be shiny not cloudy. When fish is fresh, its deliciousness speaks for itself—so one of my favorite ways to let it shine is by simply dressing it with fresh citrus, good-quality olive oil, and Maldon salt. When buying fish to be served raw, always ask for "sushi grade," which simply means that the fish is extremely fresh and good quality, thus safe for raw consumption.

LIME DRESSING

Zest of ½ lime plus juice of 1 lime
2 tablespoons unseasoned rice vinegar
1 tablespoon honey
1 tablespoon soy sauce
1 teaspoon ginger juice (see Notes)
½ teaspoon sriracha

CILANTRO CREMA

1 cup mayonnaise
1 cup tightly packed fresh cilantro
1 jalapeño, halved, seeded, and deveined
1 tablespoon freshly squeezed lime juice
2 garlic cloves
Kosher salt and freshly ground black pepper
   to taste

CRUDO

1 pound sushi-grade tuna steak
Maldon sea salt flakes, freshly cracked black
   pepper, lime zest, microgreens, and good
   quality extra virgin olive oil, for serving
   (optional)

1. To make the dressing: In a small bowl, whisk the lime zest, lime juice, rice vinegar, honey, soy sauce, ginger juice, and sriracha. Set aside.

2. To make the cilantro crema: In the bowl of a food processor fitted with the S blade, blend the mayonnaise, cilantro, jalapeño, lime juice, garlic, kosher salt, and pepper until smooth.

3. To make the crudo: Slice the tuna fillet crosswise and against the grain ¼ inch thick. On a platter, arrange the slices, overlapping slightly. Spoon the lime dressing over the fish and sprinkle with Maldon sea salt. Serve with the cilantro crema on the side.

Notes

- *To make ginger juice, use a Microplane to grate a piece of fresh ginger. Squeeze the grated pulp to release the juice. Discard the solids after squeezing out all the liquid.*

- *To keep the fish fresh, store the fillet in a zip-top bag over a tray of ice in the back of the fridge until ready to use. For easy slicing, freeze the fish and take it out of the freezer 1 hour before serving. Slice when it's partially frozen so it's easier to get thin slices and thaw on a plate.*

Variations

- *If you're not a fan of fully raw fish, season the unsliced tuna steak liberally with salt and pepper or Tajín seasoning and sear it in a hot skillet with a tablespoon of olive oil for 1 minute on each side (or longer if you want it more well done).*

- *You can also make this dish with a raw skinless salmon fillet.*

Curried Gefilte Fish Patties
Makes 10 patties

There's a time and a place for classic carrot-topped gefilte fish (Passover for me!—see page 128). But in my house, we like to buy the frozen premade loaf and change it up with different spices. This combo, inspired by Indian cuisine, marries some of my favorite flavors of garlic, ginger, and curry powder for a unique spin on gefilte that you definitely haven't seen before!

GEFILTE FISH PATTIES

1 (22-ounce) loaf gefilte fish, defrosted

⅓ cup frozen peas, thawed

2 tablespoons unseasoned panko bread crumbs

1 extra-large egg

1-inch piece fresh ginger, peeled and minced (1 heaping teaspoon)

2 garlic cloves, minced

1 scallion (white and green parts), finely diced

1 teaspoon curry powder

Pinch of red pepper flakes

Kosher salt and freshly ground black pepper to taste

BREADING

1 cup unseasoned panko bread crumbs

1 tablespoon white sesame seeds

1 tablespoon black sesame seeds

Kosher salt and freshly ground black pepper to taste

Canola oil, for frying

CURRY-HONEY MUSTARD DIP

½ cup mayonnaise

1 tablespoon honey

1 teaspoon freshly squeezed lime juice

1 teaspoon yellow mustard

½ teaspoon curry powder

Kosher salt and freshly ground black pepper to taste

1. To make the patties: In a large bowl, combine the gefilte fish, peas, panko bread crumbs, egg, ginger, garlic, scallion, curry powder, red pepper flakes, salt, and pepper. Stir with a spoon until incorporated.

2. To prepare the breading: In a separate medium bowl, combine the panko bread crumbs, white and black sesame seeds, salt, and pepper.

3. Using a cookie scoop, scoop out ¼-cup portions of the gefilte fish batter and place them in the breading, pressing to fully coat the patties in the panko. With the palm of your hand, flatten the fish into ½-inch-thick patties.

4. In a large skillet over medium heat, heat ¼ cup of canola oil. Test the oil by adding a pinch of bread crumbs; it should bubble as soon as it hits the oil.

5. Line a baking sheet or plate with paper towels. Fry the fish in batches over medium heat, 5 minutes per side, or until golden and cooked through, adding more oil as needed. Drain the patties on the paper towel–lined plate.

6. To make the dip: In a small bowl, combine the mayonnaise, honey, lime juice, mustard, curry powder, salt, and pepper. Serve with the gefilte fish patties.

Note
The fish patties may be served warm or cold. To freeze, store in a zip-top bag and freeze for up to 2 months.

Freezer-Friendly

Just
Wing
It

Pad Chai

Serves 6

This recipe fuses two of my favorite cuisines, Thai and Middle Eastern (*chai* in Hebrew means "life"). I'll never forget the first pad Thai I ever had. It was in the kosher culinary school I attended, and my mouth was on FIRE. We had made our own chili paste as the base of the sauce, and it was hottttt—but I couldn't get enough of the sour, salty, and spicy combo. In this completely untraditional hybrid recipe, I add sweet silan and spicy harissa, which pair wonderfully with the sour tamarind paste, and top it off with crushed Bamba, the most popular Israeli peanut snack, for good measure!

SAUCE

3 tablespoons silan (date honey)

¼ cup soy sauce

2 tablespoons tamarind concentrate

2 tablespoons freshly squeezed lime juice

1 teaspoon Smoky Harissa (page 303 or store-bought), or to taste

NOODLES

10 ounces pad Thai rice noodles (or linguini)

2½ tablespoons peanut oil, divided (you can also use grapeseed or canola oil)

2 pounds boneless, skinless chicken thighs, cut into bite-size pieces (or protein of your choice)

Kosher salt and freshly ground black pepper to taste

1 cup fresh bean sprouts, plus more for garnish

1 carrot, peeled and julienned

1 red bell pepper, julienned

3 garlic cloves, minced

3 extra-large eggs, beaten

3 scallions, white and green parts, sliced on the bias into 1-inch pieces

Cilantro, crushed Bamba, chopped roasted peanuts, lime wedges, for serving

1. To make the sauce: In a medium bowl, whisk together the silan, soy sauce, tamarind concentrate, lime juice, and harissa (or shake together in a mason jar). Set aside.

2. To make the noodles: Cook the noodles according to the package instructions. Drain and rinse with cold water briefly to keep them from sticking.

3. In a large sauté pan or wok over high heat, heat 1 tablespoon of the peanut oil. Add the chicken, salt, and pepper and sauté for 3 to 5 minutes, tossing occasionally, until the chicken is cooked through. Use a slotted spoon to transfer the chicken to a clean plate and set aside.

4. Add 1 more tablespoon of the peanut oil to the sauté pan along with the bean sprouts, carrot, bell pepper, and garlic. Season with salt and pepper. Sauté over high heat for 2 minutes, until the vegetables are softened. Transfer the vegetables to the plate with the chicken.

5. Add the remaining ½ tablespoon peanut oil to the pan and add the eggs, stirring frequently and seasoning with a pinch of salt and pepper, until the eggs are scrambled.

6. Return the chicken and vegetables to the pan. Add the rice noodles, scallions, and the sauce and stir until everything is evenly coated.

7. Transfer the noodles to a serving dish. Garnish with bean sprouts, cilantro, crushed Bamba, and chopped peanuts. Serve immediately with lime wedges.

Notes

- *This dish is best served immediately as the rice noodles absorb the sauce as it sits. You can double the sauce if you like.*

- *If using tamarind paste with added sugar, adjust sweetness by adding less silan.*

Instant Paprikash

Serves 6

I'm a big fan of my Instant Pot for last-minute meals, especially when I forget to take things out of the freezer. I love that it can cook solid frozen chicken in just 25 minutes! This paprikash comes together really quickly in a multicooker for a simple yet flavorful dinner on busy days. The peas aren't traditional, but when served with a grain, it makes for a balanced meal.

2 tablespoons extra-virgin olive oil

1 Spanish onion, thinly sliced into half-moons

4 garlic cloves, minced

¼ cup sweet paprika

1 plum tomato, diced

1 cup chicken or vegetable stock

6 skin-on chicken legs

Kosher salt and freshly ground black pepper to taste

10 ounces frozen peas (optional)

White or brown rice, Israeli couscous, farfel, barley, nokerlach (dumplings), or spaetzli, for serving

1. Set the Instant Pot to the Sauté setting. Pour in the olive oil and sauté the onions for 6 minutes, stirring occasionally, or until the onions are translucent. Add the garlic and continue to sauté for 1 minute, or until the garlic is fragrant and softened. Add the paprika and cook 1 more minute, until fragrant. Stir in the tomatoes and chicken stock and scrape up any stuck-on bits from the bottom of the pot.

2. Season the chicken generously with salt and pepper on both sides. Add the chicken to the pot, using a spoon to coat all the pieces in the sauce. Cover the pot with the lid and lock in place.

3. Set the Instant Pot to 15 minutes on high pressure for raw chicken or 25 minutes for frozen chicken. Turn on the Keep Warm setting.

4. When the pressure is released, add the frozen peas (if using), and cover the pot for 5 minutes, until the peas are thawed and bright green. Serve spooned over rice or the starch of your choosing.

Note

If you don't have an Instant Pot, follow the recipe until you get to the step with the chicken (you must use defrosted chicken) and then braise the chicken in a heavy-bottomed pot or Dutch oven on the stovetop over low heat for 1 hour. Or, to make it in a slow cooker: In a frying pan over medium heat, sauté the onion in the oil until the onion is translucent. Add the paprika and diced tomato and cook for 5 minutes, or until the tomatoes are softened. Place the chicken in the slow cooker and top with the onion mixture (omit the stock). Cook on low for 6 to 8 hours, until the chicken is fall-off-the-bone tender. Add the peas just before serving and cook for 2 minutes, or until just cooked through.

Yemenite "Soup" Sheet Pan Chicken

Serves 4 to 6

The only way to describe a bowl of Yemenite soup is otherworldly. The smell—a heady blend of cumin, coriander, cardamom, and cloves—intoxicates the senses. It's pure comfort food in a bowl. That smell comes from hawaij, a curry blend native to Yemenite cuisine, not to be confused with hawaij for coffee, its sweet counterpart. I use the spice blend on a whole chicken and roast it on a sheet pan for all the comfort of a bowl of soup turned into a heavenly sheet pan dinner. For the full experience, serve with schug and hilbe, a fenugreek dip traditionally served alongside the soup.

1 (3-pound) whole chicken

1 bunch of fresh cilantro

2 heads garlic, cut in half crosswise

½ lemon

1½ to 2 pounds baby Yukon gold potatoes, halved

2 plum tomatoes, quartered

1 small Spanish onion, sliced into wedges

3 tablespoons Hawaij for Soup (page 304)

¼ cup extra-virgin olive oil

Kosher salt

Hilbe and schug (page 301), for serving (optional)

1. Preheat the oven to 400°F. Line a baking sheet with parchment paper or foil.

2. Stuff the chicken cavity with most of the cilantro (reserving some for garnish), ½ head of the garlic, and the lemon half. Place it, breast-side up, in the center of the baking sheet. Arrange the potatoes, tomatoes, and onions around the chicken in a single layer.

3. In a small bowl, mix the hawaij and olive oil and brush it over the chicken (and under the skin) and vegetables. Season generously with salt. Tuck the remaining 2½ garlic heads, cut-side down, into the vegetables.

4. Bake for 1 hour, basting the chicken and vegetables with the pan juices halfway through, or until the chicken juices run clear and the vegetables are tender and caramelized.

5. Garnish with remaining fresh cilantro and serve with hilbe or schug.

Easy Does It!

Use store-bought hawaij seasoning, available in Middle Eastern markets. Pereg is my preferred brand, labeled "mixed spices for soup."

Grilled Chicken, Two Ways

Serves 6

There's nothing like a juicy, charred piece of grilled chicken, and not just for summer barbecues—I love it in the winter, too, because it's healthy and makes for a quick and easy dinner. When it's too cold to grill, I just use my broiler, which I consider an inverted grill. A grill pan works as well!

BASIL LIME GRILLED CHICKEN BREASTS

¼ cup olive oil

1 garlic clove, minced

¼ cup finely chopped fresh basil or 5 store-bought frozen basil cubes

Zest and juice of 1 lime

1 tablespoon honey

½ teaspoon red pepper flakes

1 teaspoon kosher salt

¼ teaspoon freshly ground black pepper

2 pounds boneless, skinless chicken breast, cut into 1-inch pieces

LEMON SUMAC GRILLED CHICKEN THIGHS

¼ cup grapeseed oil

2 garlic cloves, minced

Zest and juice of ½ lemon

2 tablespoons silan (date honey)

2 teaspoons ground sumac

1 teaspoon kosher salt

¼ teaspoon freshly ground black pepper

2 pounds boneless, skinless chicken thighs, cut into 1-inch pieces

1. Marinate the chicken: If making the Basil-Lime Grilled Chicken Breasts, to a gallon-size zip-top bag, combine the olive oil, garlic, basil, lime zest and juice, honey, red pepper flakes, salt, and pepper. If making the Lemon-Sumac Grilled Chicken Thighs, to a zip-top bag, combine the grapeseed oil, garlic, lemon zest and juice, silan, salt, and pepper. Add the chicken, seal the bag, and marinate in the fridge for 1 hour.

2. Soak six wooden skewers in water while the chicken marinates or use metal skewers.

3. When the chicken is finished marinating, thread the chicken onto the skewers, about 8 pieces per skewer.

4. Adjust an oven rack to the highest position and preheat the broiler to high, or heat a charcoal or gas grill to high heat. If grilling, grease the grates with oil or brush an indoor grill pan with oil. Broil or grill for 5 minutes per side for chicken breasts and 8 minutes per side for chicken thighs, until the chicken is charred and no longer pink.

Note

You can also grill whole pieces of chicken, if desired.

Chicken and "Waffle" Drumsticks with Hot Maple Syrup

Serves 8

When I was a kid, my mom always made drumsticks for us because they were fun and easy to eat. She would wrap the bone in a napkin, and we'd eat them Flintstone-style. In my house, we call them lollipops, and we top them with all sorts of fun breadings. It doesn't get better than this sugar cone–coated number with hot maple syrup. It's a sweet and salty dream! Yabba Dabba Doo!

CONE CRUMBS
1 (6-ounce) package sugar cones
2 teaspoons smoked paprika
2 teaspoons kosher salt

FLOUR
½ cup all-purpose flour
½ teaspoon kosher salt
¼ teaspoon freshly ground black pepper

EGGS
2 extra-large eggs, beaten
¼ teaspoon kosher salt
⅛ teaspoon freshly ground black pepper

DRUMSTICKS
12 skin-on chicken drumsticks
Maldon sea salt flakes, for finishing

HOT MAPLE SYRUP
½ cup maple syrup
2 teaspoons sriracha
1 tablespoon bourbon (optional)

1. Preheat the oven to 400°F. Line a baking sheet with parchment paper and grease the parchment with cooking spray.

2. Roughly crush the sugar cones and place them in the bowl of a food processor fitted with the S blade with smoked paprika and salt. Pulse the cones into small bits and transfer to a shallow bowl.

3. In a second shallow bowl, place the flour, and into a third shallow bowl, add the eggs. Season the flour and eggs with salt and pepper.

4. Working with one chicken drumstick at a time, roll the drumsticks in the flour so all sides are well coated, tapping off any excess. Dip the drumsticks in the egg and let any excess drip off. Finally, roll the drumsticks in the sugar cone crumbs, pressing so the crumbs stick to the chicken. After breading, place each drumstick on the prepared baking sheet.

5. Spray the chicken with cooking spray. Bake for 40 to 45 minutes, until the breading is crispy and starting to brown and the chicken is cooked through.

6. While the chicken roasts, make the syrup: In a small bowl, combine the maple syrup with the sriracha. Stir in the bourbon (if using).

7. Remove the chicken from the oven, brush or drizzle with the syrup, and sprinkle with Maldon sea salt to finish. Serve immediately.

Cabbage and Apple Roast Chicken
Serves 6

Cabbage and apples go together like peanut butter and jelly, and when paired with a chicken that's smothered in sweet and spicy mustard, you end up with a one-pan dinner that you'll definitely make on repeat!

6 bone-in, skin-on chicken thighs
½ head green or red cabbage, cut into 8 wedges
2 apples, cored, cut in quarters
Kosher salt and freshly ground black pepper to taste
2 tablespoons Dijon mustard
2 tablespoons whole-grain mustard
¼ cup maple syrup
2 garlic cloves, minced
2 teaspoons chopped fresh thyme leaves
2 tablespoons extra-virgin olive oil

1. Preheat the oven to 425°F. Line a baking sheet with parchment paper.

2. Arrange the chicken, cabbage, and apples on the baking sheet. Season liberally with salt and pepper.

3. In a small bowl, whisk together the Dijon, whole-grain mustard, maple syrup, garlic, and thyme. Brush the mixture over the chicken and under its skin and over the cabbage and apples. Drizzle the olive oil over the chicken, cabbage, and apples. Bake for 45 minutes, until the chicken skin is crispy and the cabbage and apples are caramelized.

Variation

You can also use boneless, skinless chicken thighs. Reduce the baking time to 25 to 30 minutes, and roast until the chicken is crispy around the edges and no longer pink.

Spatchcock Sesame Chicken

Serves 4

I don't just make spatchcock chicken because it's fun to say—this method of butterflying a chicken so that it lays flat actually results in a more evenly cooked bird with extra crispy skin all around plus a faster cooking time too. I smother it in sesame seeds à la Israeli-style sesame challah (see Shlissel Jerusalem Bagel, page 53), giving it a sweet and nutty crunch that is sublime! Don't skip the chili crisp here. It takes the chicken to the next level.

1 (3-pound) whole chicken
6 tablespoons white sesame seeds
2 tablespoons black sesame seeds
1 teaspoon kosher salt
1 teaspoon red pepper flakes
1 extra-large egg white
1 teaspoon soy sauce
Sliced chives or scallion tops, for serving
Chili Crisp (page 294), for serving

1. Preheat the oven to 375°F. Line a baking sheet with parchment paper.

2. To spatchcock the chicken (also known as butterflying), place the whole chicken on a clean cutting board, breast-side down. Starting at the thigh end, cut along one side of the backbone with kitchen shears all the way up to the neck. Cut along the other side of the backbone up to the neck to remove the backbone. Discard the backbone or freeze it in a resealable zip-top bag for chicken soup or stock. Flip the chicken over and open it like a book. Press firmly on the breast bone with the heels of your hands to flatten. (You should hear a small crack or pop when the breast bone cracks, allowing the chicken to lie flat.)

3. In a small bowl, combine the white and black sesame seeds, salt, and red pepper flakes. In a second small bowl, whisk together the egg white and soy sauce.

4. Place the chicken, skin-side up, on the baking sheet. Using a pastry brush, brush the egg white mixture over the chicken. Sprinkle the chicken generously with the sesame seed mixture so that it's fully coated. Bake, uncovered, for 50 minutes, until a thermometer inserted into the thigh registers 165°F and the chicken juices run clear. Garnish with the chives and serve with the Chili Crisp.

Note

If you find it difficult to spatchcock the chicken, ask your butcher to butterfly the chicken for you, or just use a quartered chicken instead.

Italian Chicken and Orzo Bake

Serves 6

I was lucky enough to travel to Italy in the summer of 2021 to experience its breathtaking landscapes, unparalleled produce, and unforgettable food and culture. When I returned to Brooklyn from my trip, I knew I had to include a recipe inspired by my travels in this book. I decided to use the beautiful sundried tomatoes, dried oregano, and pepperoncini flakes I had purchased in the farmers' market in Rome. Enriched with lemon slices (purchased in Brooklyn!) and packed with sunny flavor, this recipe will transport you to the Amalfi coast.

3 tablespoons extra-virgin olive oil, divided

6 bone-in, skin-on chicken thighs

Kosher salt and freshly ground black pepper to taste

2 lemons, sliced, divided

½ cup sundried tomatoes, sliced ¼ inch thick

3 garlic cloves, minced

2 teaspoons dried oregano

½ teaspoon pepperoncini flakes or ¼ teaspoon red pepper flakes

⅓ cup dry white wine

2 cups uncooked orzo

4 cups chicken stock

Fresh parsley or basil, chopped, for serving

1. Preheat the oven to 350°F.

2. In a large Dutch oven over high heat, heat 1 tablespoon of the olive oil. Season the chicken liberally with salt and pepper on both sides and add to the pot. Sear for 5 minutes per side, or until golden brown on each side. Use tongs to remove the chicken thighs from the pot and set them on a plate. In the same pot, sear the slices from 1 of the lemons until caramelized and set them aside with the chicken.

3. Pour the remaining 2 tablespoons olive oil into the pot (if there is rendered fat from the chicken, omit some of the olive oil). Chop the remaining lemon slices into pieces and add them to the pot with the sundried tomatoes. Sauté over medium heat for 6 minutes, stirring constantly with a wooden spoon, or until the lemon starts to caramelize. Add the garlic and sauté for 1 minute, until fragrant. Add the oregano and pepperoncini flakes and stir for 1 minute, or until fragrant.

4. Add the white wine, scraping up any stuck-on bits from the bottom of the pot, and cook for 2 minutes, or until the wine is mostly evaporated. Add the orzo and stir for 5 minutes, or until lightly toasted. Stir in the chicken stock to incorporate.

5. Return the chicken to the pot and top with reserved lemon slices, cover, and transfer to the oven for 50 minutes, until the chicken is cooked through. Garnish with parsley before serving.

Notes

- *To make this in a 9 × 13-inch baking dish or disposable aluminum pan, spread the orzo on the bottom of the pan. Sear the chicken in a large skillet and place on top of the orzo. Prepare the sauce in the skillet as above and pour over the chicken and orzo. Cover with foil and bake for 50 to 60 minutes, until the chicken is cooked through and the liquid is absorbed.*

- *If you find lemon rind too bitter, you can blanch the lemon slices by adding it to a pot of boiling water for 2 minutes. Remove with a slotted spoon and drain on paper towels before searing. Or skip adding the chopped lemon in step 3 and just serve with sliced lemon in step 5.*

Turkey Roast with Za'atar Gravy

Serves 6 to 8

When a giant turkey feels like too much of a hassle, but you're craving all the Thanksgiving feels, a turkey roast makes a great stand-in. The luscious lemony za'atar gravy isn't your traditional holiday fix, but paired with Tahini Pumpkin Pie (page 244) and pomegranate-sumac cranberry sauce (see page 187), you'll have lots to be thankful for!

TURKEY ROAST

1 lemon

3 tablespoons za'atar

3 tablespoons extra-virgin olive oil

3 garlic cloves, minced

3-pound white meat turkey roast

Kosher salt and freshly ground black pepper to taste

⅓ cup dry white wine

ZA'ATAR GRAVY

2 cups chicken stock

1 tablespoon za'atar

1 to 2 tablespoons honey

2 tablespoons cornstarch

Kosher salt and freshly ground black pepper to taste

1. Preheat the oven to 350°F.

2. To make the turkey roast: Into a small bowl, zest the lemon. Slice the lemon into ⅛-inch-thick rounds and set aside. To the bowl with the zest, add the za'atar, olive oil, and garlic. Rub the mixture over the turkey breast and place it in a Dutch oven. Season the turkey liberally with salt and pepper. Place the sliced lemons in the pot around the turkey and then add the wine.

3. Bake, covered, for 1 hour, until the turkey is opaque. Uncover, raise the oven temperature to 400°F, and bake for an additional 30 minutes, until a thermometer inserted into the thickest part of the breast measures 160°F.

4. Use tongs to remove the turkey from the pot and transfer it to a plate; tent the roast with foil and allow it to rest for 10 minutes. Pour any juices that collect on the plate back into the pot. Use a slotted spoon to remove the lemons from the pot and set aside (you'll use them for garnish).

5. To make the gravy: Into the Dutch oven, pour the chicken stock and bring it to a simmer over medium heat, using a wooden spoon to scrape up any stuck-on bits from the pot. Add the za'atar and honey.

6. In a small bowl, combine the cornstarch with 2 tablespoons water and whisk until smooth. Pour the cornstarch slurry into the pot and whisk until thickened. Season with salt and pepper. Adjust the seasoning by adding more honey if the gravy is too tart. For extra-smooth gravy, strain if desired.

7. To serve, slice the turkey and serve with gravy alongside or spooned over the top. Garnish with reserved lemon slices.

Freezer-Friendly

To freeze, wrap the sliced turkey in foil and place in a zip-top bag. Transfer the gravy to an airtight container and freeze for up to 2 months.

Split Hooves

(+ chews its cud!)

Taco Tuesday Pasta !

Serves 6

Taco Tuesday is a favorite among busy moms, especially when you buy the taco kit in the store with the ready-made seasoning mix. Ground beef cooks up super fast, and dinner is on the table in under 20 minutes. This elevated version comes together in just about the same amount of time, with the pasta cooking directly in the sauce. Have fun with different pasta shapes, and take your Taco Tuesday game to the next level.

2 tablespoons extra-virgin olive oil

1 large Spanish onion, diced

2 garlic cloves, minced

2 pounds ground beef (not lean)

2 tablespoons tomato paste

1½ tablespoons ground cumin

1½ teaspoons smoked paprika

2 teaspoons chili powder

1 teaspoon dried oregano

1 teaspoon garlic powder

1 cup canned black beans, rinsed and drained

1 (15-ounce) can diced tomatoes

7 ounces canned corn, drained

2 teaspoons kosher salt

⅛ teaspoon freshly ground black pepper

1 pound rigatoni (or your favorite pasta)

Vegan sour cream and chopped cilantro
   for serving (optional)

1. In an 8-quart pot over medium heat, heat the olive oil. Add the onion and sauté for 5 minutes, or until translucent. Add the garlic and continue to sauté for 1 minute, or until fragrant. Stir in the ground beef and cook for 6 minutes, breaking it up as it cooks, or until browned and crumbled. Drain and discard the rendered fat from the pot.

2. Add the tomato paste and continue to sauté for 3 minutes, or until it darkens. Add the cumin, smoked paprika, chili powder, oregano, and garlic powder and sauté for 2 minutes, or until fragrant. Stir in the beans, tomatoes, corn, salt, pepper, and 4 cups water. Bring the mixture to a simmer over high heat.

3. Add the pasta, cover the pot, reduce the heat to medium, and simmer 12 to 14 minutes, stirring halfway through, until the pasta is cooked completely. Serve with vegan sour cream and cilantro, if desired.

Easy Does It!

Use a package of prepared taco mix in place of the spices.

Burger Bowls with Umami Burger Bombs

Serves 6 to 8

These little bites of heaven go against everything I believe in when making a burger: (1) don't handle the meat, (2) season it with just salt and pepper, and (3) never ever use onion soup mix. Except... I had this idea of flavoring the meat with all the umami-rich ingredients I could think of, and they were just *that good* that none of the above mattered. I love to make the burgers into little bite-size "bombs" and divide them among bowls, adding all the components you would find in a burger. The special sauce is a combination of all the burger condiments you can think of—but it comes together in such a delicious spread that you'll want to put it on everything!

BURGERS

2 pounds ground beef (for best results, do not use lean)
2 tablespoons onion soup mix
4 teaspoons soy sauce
4 teaspoons tomato paste
2 teaspoons umami spice or porcini mushroom powder

BOWLS

6 ounces beef bacon
½ head iceberg lettuce, shredded
2 beefsteak tomatoes, sliced
1 small red onion, halved and thinly sliced into half-moons
½ cup bread-and-butter pickles
½ (26-ounce) bag frozen crinkle-cut fries, cooked according to package directions

SPECIAL SAUCE

⅓ cup mayonnaise
3 tablespoons ketchup
2 tablespoons barbecue sauce
1 tablespoon yellow mustard
1 tablespoon pickle relish
1 teaspoon freshly squeezed lemon juice

1. Preheat the oven to 425°F.

2. To make the burgers: Line a baking sheet with foil and place a baking rack over it. In a large bowl, combine the ground beef, onion soup mix, soy sauce, tomato paste, and umami spice and mix until incorporated (try not to handle the meat too much). Divide the burger mixture into 2-tablespoon torpedo-shaped portions and place them on the rack. Bake for 8 to 10 minutes, until the meat is juicy and browned.

3. To cook the bacon: Line a second baking sheet with parchment paper. Place the beef bacon on the baking sheet in a single layer and bake for 15 minutes (on the rack below the burgers), until crispy.

4. To make the special sauce: In a small bowl, whisk together the mayonnaise, ketchup, barbecue sauce, mustard, relish, and lemon juice.

5. To assemble the bowls, divide the burger bombs, lettuce, tomatoes, onions, pickles, beef bacon, and fries among the bowls. Drizzle with the special sauce.

Freezer-Friendly

You can freeze leftover burger bombs in a zip-top bag for up to 3 months. Thaw and warm in a 350°F oven until heated through.

Cowboy Steak for Two

Serves 2

When it comes to cooking meat, there are two basic preparation methods: dry-roasting to a specific doneness (see Guidelines below) or braising in a liquid until pull-apart tender. Me? I'm a dry-roasting gal. I love the texture of a perfectly medium-rare steak, and I find it less heavy than its braised counterpart. The simplicity in its preparation is just the cherry on the top! Paired with a glass of dry red wine, this is my ultimate treat.

1 cowboy rib-eye steak (see Note)
Kosher salt and freshly ground black pepper to taste
1 tablespoon grapeseed oil
2 sprigs of fresh rosemary or thyme
3 garlic cloves, unpeeled
Chimichurri (page 301) for serving (optional)

MEAT TEMPERATURE GUIDELINES:

very rare (sometimes referred to as "blue" meat) 115°–120°F

rare (deep red center) 120°–130°F

medium-rare (bright red center) 130°–140°F

medium (pink center) 140°–150°F

medium-well (very little pink) 150°–160°F

well-done (all brown) 160°F +

1. Allow the steak to come to room temperature for 1 hour. Pat dry with a paper towel and season generously with salt and pepper. In a cast-iron or heavy-bottomed skillet over medium-high heat, heat the grapeseed oil until it's shimmering.

2. Place the steak in the skillet along with the rosemary and garlic and cook for 5 minutes on one side without touching. Use a spatula to press down on the steak so it develops a nice crust. Flip the steak and cook for 5 more minutes on the other side. Use tongs to lift the steak by the bone and sear the sides of the steak, allowing the fat to render, 2 more minutes per side.

3. Use a meat thermometer to check for doneness (I prefer 130–135°F), keeping in mind that the temperature will continue to rise about 10°F after you remove the steak from the heat and it rests. Transfer the steak to a 400°F oven and continue to cook until desired temperature is reached, about 10 to 20 minutes.

4. Transfer the steak to a plate or cutting board, and allow to rest for 10 minutes before slicing or serving. Slice against the grain and serve with the garlic and rosemary from the skillet and chimichurri, if desired.

Note

A cowboy steak is a thick-cut bone-in rib-eye steak with a thickness of 2 to 2½ inches.

Variation

To grill the steak, preheat one side of the grill to high heat and leave the other side off. Grease the grates. Grill the steak for 5 minutes per side over high heat, then transfer to indirect heat, cover and grill for an additional 10 to 20 minutes, or until desired temperature is reached (see Guidelines).

Miso London Broil
Serves 6

London broil is one of my favorite budget-friendly cuts of meat, perfect for weeknight dinner yet flavorful enough for a fancy affair *if* you cook it right. Technically, London broil is not an actual cut of meat but rather a cooking method—meaning that the meat is marinated and then grilled or broiled. It's typically made with cuts from the shoulder, with the shoulder blade or split brick roast being my favorite. When marinated in a flavorful rub that includes umami-rich miso paste and sweet and salty gochujang (a Korean fermented chili paste), then grilled to medium-rare and sliced thinly against the grain, it rivals many a more expensive cut.

⅓ cup white (shiro) miso paste

3 tablespoons maple syrup

1 heaping tablespoon gochujang chili paste or 2 teaspoons sriracha (see Note on page 198)

2 tablespoons unseasoned rice vinegar

¼ cup grapeseed oil

½ teaspoon coarsely ground black pepper

10 ounces large shiitake mushrooms (see Variation)

2½ pounds London broil (flat cut such as shoulder blade or split brick)

1. In a small bowl, combine the miso paste, maple syrup, gochujang, rice vinegar, grapeseed oil, 3 tablespoons water, and the pepper. Whisk until smooth.

2. In a gallon-size zip-top bag, combine the marinade, London broil, and mushrooms, lightly massage to coat thoroughly, and marinate in the fridge for 2 hours.

3. Preheat the broiler to high with the oven rack in the highest position. Place the London broil and mushrooms on a baking sheet with the marinade. Broil for 6 to 8 minutes, until the meat is starting to crisp up around the edges. Turn the meat over, stir the mushrooms, and broil for an additional 6 to 8 minutes for medium-rare doneness. Remove the pan from the oven and rest for 10 minutes. Thinly slice crosswise against the grain. Transfer to a platter.

4. Place the baking sheet over medium heat on the stovetop. Stir the mushrooms with the sauce from the pan, scraping up any bits from around the pan with a spatula. If the sauce is very thick, add a bit of hot water to thin it out. Spread the sauce over the meat and serve.

Note

For best results, use a heavy-duty nondisposable sheet pan.

Variations

- *Try using other mushrooms, such as baby bella or oyster.*

- *You can also grill the London Broil for approximately 6 to 8 minutes per side. Roast the mushrooms separately with the marinade in the oven at 425°F degrees, stirring occasionally, until tender, 15 to 20 minutes.*

Maple Chipotle Chili with Pumpkin Corn Muffins

Serves 8 to 10

I developed a variation of this recipe for a pop-up I did with a chef friend in my neighborhood. It was early winter, and I wanted a stick-to-your-ribs kind of recipe that warmed you up from the inside out. The addition of smoky chipotle in the corn bread complements the chili perfectly, while the pumpkin keeps them extra-moist. Needless to say, we sold out to rave reviews.

6 ounces beef bacon, chopped into 1-inch pieces

3 pounds beef chuck roast, cubed

½ cup all-purpose flour

2 teaspoons kosher salt, divided

1 teaspoon freshly ground black pepper

1 tablespoon extra-virgin olive oil

1 large Spanish onion, diced

4 garlic cloves, minced

3 tablespoons tomato paste

½ cup beef, chicken, or vegetable stock

2 (14.5-ounce) cans fire-roasted diced tomatoes

1 chipotle pepper in adobo sauce, finely chopped

2 tablespoons adobo sauce

3 tablespoons maple syrup

2 tablespoons apple cider vinegar

1 tablespoon ground cumin

1 tablespoon smoked paprika

2 teaspoons dried oregano

Vegan sour cream and cilantro, for serving

1. In a Dutch oven over medium heat, cook the bacon for 6 minutes, or until crispy, and remove it from the pan.

2. In a medium bowl, combine the flour with 1 teaspoon of the salt and ½ teaspoon of the black pepper and toss to coat the beef cubes. Add the cubes to the Dutch oven and sauté in the bacon drippings for 7 to 8 minutes, cooking until the beef is crispy and browned and stirring as needed. Remove from the heat and set aside.

3. Pour the olive oil into the pan and let heat for a minute. Add the onion and garlic and sauté for 5 minutes, or until browned and fragrant. Add the tomato paste and cook for another 3 minutes, or until the tomato paste is dark red and the aromatics have softened.

4. Reserve ¼ cup of the cooked bacon and set aside. Add the remaining bacon, beef, stock, diced tomatoes with their juices, chipotle pepper, adobo sauce, maple syrup, vinegar, cumin, paprika, oregano, and the remaining 1 teaspoon salt and ½ teaspoon black pepper. Use a wooden spoon to scrape up any crispy bits from the bottom of the pan. Bring the mixture to a simmer over medium heat. Reduce the heat and cook, covered, for 1½ hours, until the meat is tender.

5. Serve warm, topped with the reserved beef bacon crumbles, Pumpkin Corn Muffins (recipe follows), vegan sour cream, and cilantro.

Note

This chili is on the spicy side, but you can reduce the chipotle pepper and adobo sauce (in the chili and muffins) to make it more kid-friendly.

Variation

You can also make this recipe using 3 pounds of ground beef instead of the chuck. Omit step 2 and brown the meat instead, remove from the pot, and continue with step 3.

Freezer-Friendly

PUMPKIN CORN MUFFINS
Makes 24 muffins

1½ cups all-purpose flour
1½ cups yellow cornmeal
½ cup sugar
2 teaspoons baking powder
1 teaspoon chipotle chile powder
1½ teaspoons kosher salt
1 teaspoon ground cinnamon
½ teaspoon baking soda
2 tablespoons maple syrup
1 cup coconut milk
½ cup canola oil
2 extra-large eggs
1 (15-ounce) can pumpkin (not pumpkin pie filling)

1. Preheat the oven to 350°F. Spray two muffin tins with cooking spray.

2. In a large bowl, whisk together the flour, cornmeal, sugar, baking powder, chili powder, salt, cinnamon, and baking soda. In a separate medium bowl, whisk together the maple syrup, coconut milk, oil, and eggs. Pour the wet ingredients into the dry ingredients and stir with a spoon to incorporate. Add the pumpkin and mix to combine.

3. Divide the batter among the muffin cups, filling each three-quarters full. Bake for 25 minutes, until a toothpick inserted into the center of a muffin comes out clean.

Note

1 teaspoon smoked paprika and a pinch of cayenne pepper can be swapped for chipotle chile powder.

Pucker-Up Ribs
Serves 6

I'm not a big candy person, but I can get down with super-sour candy that makes my mouth pucker. That's why I love fresh cranberries—they're like nature's Cry Baby candies! I rev up the tartness in the cranberry sauce here with naturally tangy sumac, pomegranate juice, and lemon for a mouth-puckering experience you're going to love!

POMEGRANATE-SUMAC CRANBERRY SAUCE

12 ounces fresh or frozen cranberries (thawed, if frozen)

1 cup pomegranate juice

½ cup honey

2 teaspoons ground sumac

Zest and juice of 1 lemon

RIBS

3 pounds bone-in beef spare ribs

Kosher salt and freshly ground black pepper to taste

3 tablespoons grapeseed oil

1. Preheat the oven to 500°F.

2. To make the cranberry sauce: In a medium saucepan, add the cranberries, pomegranate juice, honey, sumac, lemon zest, and lemon juice and set over medium-high heat. Bring the mixture to a boil, reduce the heat so the sauce is at a gentle simmer, and cook, uncovered, for 25 minutes, stirring occasionally, until the sauce is thickened and coats the back of a spoon.

3. While the sauce reduces, prepare the ribs: In a large baking dish, place the ribs and season them generously with salt and pepper on both sides. Drizzle with the oil and roast for 10 minutes per side, until each side is browned.

4. Reduce the oven temperature to 325°F. Pour the cranberry sauce over the ribs and cover with two layers of foil. Bake for 2 hours, until the meat is fork-tender and the ribs are falling off the bone. Remove from the oven and transfer to a platter to serve.

Note
You can also use this recipe to prepare short ribs, flanken ribs, or back ribs.

Freezer-Friendly
To freeze the ribs, transfer them to a 9 × 13-inch disposable pan and cover with two layers of foil. Freeze for up to 3 months. When ready to use, defrost in the refrigerator overnight, then heat in a 300°F oven until warmed through, about 25 minutes.

Slow Cooker Berbere Brisket
Serves 6 to 8

Berbere is the flavor backbone of Ethiopian cooking. It's a spice blend made from chiles, garlic, fenugreek, and a handful of warm spices, such as allspice and cinnamon. It beautifully seasons beef or chicken and can also be used to add flavor to stews, chili, lentils, beans, and grains. The fiery, sweet, and spicy rub puts a new spin on Texas-style dry-rubbed brisket, and with my simple slow cooker preparation, you can set it and forget it! Here, I make my own berbere blend that I've based on my flavor preferences. Feel free to adjust it to your liking or shortcut it and buy the premade blend in your grocery store. In addition to serving as a centerpiece dish with rice or flatbread, you can also stuff the meat into tortillas for tacos or add it to a slider roll.

3 tablespoons hot paprika

1 tablespoon dried minced onion flakes

2 teaspoons kosher salt

1 teaspoon ground cumin

1 teaspoon ground coriander

1 teaspoon ground cardamom

½ teaspoon granulated garlic

½ teaspoon ground ginger

½ teaspoon coarsely ground black pepper

¼ teaspoon ground allspice

¼ teaspoon ground cinnamon

¼ teaspoon ground cloves

3 pounds brisket (preferably second cut)

Orange Cardamom Rice (page 234) or injera (traditional Ethiopian flatbread), lachuch (Yemenite flabread), or laffa, for serving

1. In a small bowl, mix together the paprika, onion flakes, salt, cumin, coriander, cardamom, garlic, ginger, pepper, allspice, cinnamon, and cloves. Rub the spices onto both sides of the brisket. Wrap the brisket tightly in foil with the fattier side facing up.

2. Place the brisket in the slow cooker and set on low. Cover and cook for 8 hours, until the meat is tender and a fork slides through easily.

3. Remove the foil packet from the slow cooker. Unwrap the brisket and transfer it to a cutting board. Transfer the juices that accumulated in the foil packet to a small bowl. Slice the brisket crosswise against the grain or use two forks to pull it apart. Serve over rice or stuff it into injera, lachuch, or laffa with the pan juices.

Variation

To cook the brisket in the oven, place the dry-rubbed brisket in a roasting pan (do not enclose it in foil), add enough beef stock to fill the pan by about ½ inch, cover the pan tightly with foil, and bake at 325°F for 4 to 6 hours, until fork-tender. Proceed with the recipe as written.

Freezer-Friendly

Delmonico Roast with Balsamic Onion Petals

Serves 6

This recipe was inspired by a fabulous balsamic onion jam that a friend gifted me. Its sweet and acidic flavors paired wonderfully with steak and good-quality Dijon, so I used the flavor profile as inspiration for this roast, which you can braise for a soft, buttery bite or roast for that chewy medium-rare texture.

4 tablespoons extra-virgin olive oil, divided

2 tablespoons Dijon mustard

1 tablespoon chopped fresh rosemary

3 garlic cloves, minced

1½ teaspoons kosher salt, divided

1½ teaspoons coarsely ground black pepper, divided

1 (3-pound) Delmonico roast (see Note)

3 large red onions, quartered

3 tablespoons (packed) dark brown sugar

¼ cup dry red wine

¼ cup balsamic vinegar

1. Preheat the oven to 450°F.

2. In a small bowl, combine 2 tablespoons of the olive oil, the mustard, rosemary, garlic, 1 teaspoon of the salt, and 1 teaspoon of the pepper. Smear the mixture all over the roast and set it in a Dutch oven. Let it come to room temperature for 1 hour.

3. To braise (for a soft, melt-in-your-mouth texture): Scatter the onions around the roast. Drizzle the onions with the remaining 2 tablespoons olive oil and season with the remaining ½ teaspoon salt and ½ teaspoon pepper. Roast, uncovered, for 25 minutes, until the meat takes on some color.

4. Remove the pan from the oven. Sprinkle the brown sugar over the onions and add the red wine and vinegar. Reduce the oven temperature to 325°F. Cover the pan and bake for 2 hours, until fork-tender, flipping once halfway through. Remove the meat from the pot and set aside to cool. If desired, you can reduce the sauce to thicken before serving. To serve, slice the roast when it's completely cool. Return it to the pot to warm in the sauce, transfer to a platter, and serve.

5. To dry roast (for a medium-rare chewy texture): Prepare the roast as per step 2. In a large bowl, toss the onions with 2 tablespoons olive oil, 2 tablespoons balsamic vinegar, 2 tablespoons brown sugar, ½ teaspoon salt, and ½ teaspoon pepper. Place the roast on a baking sheet and spread the onions around the roast. Preheat the oven to 450°F and roast for 20 minutes. Reduce the oven temperature to 350°F and roast for approximately 25 minutes, or until the desired internal temperature is reached (130°F recommended). Rest for 10 minutes, slice, and serve with roasted onions (not recommended to freeze).

Note

A Delmonico roast is like the rib-eye of the chuck or shoulder portion of the steer. It is a tender cut that can be braised or dry-roasted. If you can't find that cut, you may use a brick roast, French roast, or square roast.

Freezer-Friendly

To freeze the cooked roast, let the meat cool, then slice it crosswise and against the grain. Place the meat in an airtight container with the sauce, and freeze. The night before you're ready to serve, transfer the frozen roast to the refrigerator to thaw. Transfer to an oven-safe baking dish and reheat in a 350°F oven for 25 minutes or until warmed through (this is for the braised roast; I do not recommend freezing the dry-roasted beef).

Melt-in-Your-Mouth Veal Meatballs

Serves 10

An updated version of an #oldiebutgoodie recipe from my blog, these veal meatballs truly are next-level delicious! Unlike traditional tomato-based sauces that are thick and heavy, this beer-based onion sauce is light yet richly flavorful, marrying well with the delicate veal that's flecked with citrusy notes of coriander and herbaceous fennel. I like to make the meatballs really small, like cocktail-size single-bite nibbles.

MEATBALLS

2 pounds ground veal (or dark meat ground turkey)

2 extra-large eggs

½ cup seasoned bread crumbs

1 teaspoon ground coriander

1 teaspoon kosher salt

½ teaspoon fennel seeds, crushed lightly with the bottom of a frying pan

½ teaspoon granulated garlic

½ teaspoon freshly ground black pepper

Mashed potatoes, fennel purée, cauliflower mash, or turnip mash, for serving

SAUCE

2 tablespoons extra-virgin olive oil

1 large Vidalia onion, halved and thinly sliced into half-moons

1 large fennel bulb, stalks removed, cored, and thinly sliced

2 (12-ounce) bottles pale ale

3 cups veal, chicken, or vegetable stock

5 dried bay leaves

5 sprigs of fresh thyme

⅓ cup (packed) dark brown sugar, or to taste

Kosher salt and freshly ground black pepper to taste

1. To prepare the meatballs: In a large bowl, combine the ground veal, eggs, bread crumbs, coriander, salt, fennel seeds, garlic, and pepper, mixing gently to incorporate. Set aside.

2. To make the sauce: In a 6-quart pot over medium heat, heat the olive oil. Add the onions and fennel and sauté for 25 minutes, stirring occasionally, or until deeply caramelized. Add the ale and stock and scrape up any bits from the bottom of the pot. Add the bay leaves, thyme, brown sugar, salt, and pepper and bring the mixture to a simmer.

3. Roll the meat into bite-size balls (about ½ tablespoon each) and add them to the simmering sauce. Simmer, covered, for 2 hours, until the meatballs are very soft and tender. Serve over mashed potatoes, fennel purée, cauliflower or turnip mash.

Meatless
Meals

Cauliflower Kasha Varnishkes

Serves 6

You are one of two people. If you're still reading this, you probably love the traditional Ashkenazi dish of buckwheat kasha with bow-tie pasta. Or, if you've already turned the page, chances are you have nightmares of being force-fed kasha as a kid. Thankfully, I am the former, and I couldn't resist creating a healthy spin on the classic, replacing the pasta with roasted cauliflower! You can serve this as a main dish, a side dish, or even a savory breakfast.

1 large cauliflower (3 pounds), cut into bite-size pieces

5 tablespoons extra-virgin olive oil, divided

2 teaspoons kosher salt, divided

¾ teaspoon black pepper, divided

1 large Spanish onion, thinly sliced into half-moons

1 cup kasha (buckwheat groats)

1 extra-large egg, lightly beaten

2 cups vegetable stock

Fresh parsley and dill, chopped, for garnish

Sour cream or yogurt, for serving (optional)

1. Preheat the oven to 425°F. Line a baking sheet with parchment paper.

2. Spread the cauliflower on the prepared baking sheet and toss with 2 tablespoons of the olive oil, 1 teaspoon of the salt, and ½ teaspoon of the pepper. Roast for 25 minutes, until tender and caramelized.

3. While the cauliflower is roasting, in a 10-inch sauté pan over medium heat, heat 2 tablespoons of the olive oil. Add the onions and ½ teaspoon of the salt and sauté for 25 minutes, until deeply browned and caramelized. Remove the onions from the pan and set them aside.

4. In a small bowl, stir together the kasha and the beaten egg. Mix, making sure all the grains are coated. Set the sauté pan you used for the onion on medium-high heat and add the remaining 1 tablespoon of olive oil. Transfer the kasha to the pan and flatten the mound of grains. Stir, breaking up the egg-coated kasha with a fork or wooden spoon, for 2 to 4 minutes, until the egg has dried on the kasha and the kernels brown and mostly separate. Add the stock, the remaining ½ teaspoon salt, and the remaining ¼ teaspoon pepper and bring to a boil. Cover, reduce the heat to low, and cook for 10 minutes, until all the liquid is absorbed. Remove the pan from the heat, keep covered, and steam for 10 minutes, until the kasha is fluffy.

5. When the kasha is ready, transfer it to a large bowl and combine it with the cauliflower and onions. Garnish with fresh herbs. Serve with sour cream or yogurt (if desired).

Tofu Kalbi

Serves 2

This is the recipe that finally, after many attempts, turned me on to tofu. The method for crispy frying comes from *Bon Appétit*, and the glaze is inspired by Korean barbecue-glazed short ribs called kalbi or galbi. The kosher version I've had at restaurants calls for thin slices of flanken called "Miami ribs," and the marinade often includes Asian pear, which is said to help tenderize the meat. I'm not a fan of calling tofu something it isn't—like chicken wings or ribs, so we'll just call this kalbi! I prefer to use Trader Joe's extra-firm sprouted tofu.

1 (15.5-ounce) package extra-firm sprouted tofu

⅓ cup freshly squeezed orange juice

¼ cup (packed) dark brown sugar

3 garlic cloves, minced

1-inch piece fresh ginger, peeled and grated using a rasp-style grater

3 tablespoons soy sauce

1 heaping tablespoon gochujang (see Note)

2 teaspoons toasted sesame oil

Zest of ½ lime plus juice of 1 lime

¼ cup canola oil

Prepared rice, lettuce cups, chives, Thai red chile slices, sesame seeds, and lime wedges, for serving

1. Drain the tofu, then sandwich it between several layers of paper towels. Cover the tofu with a plate, place a heavy can on top, and set aside for 30 minutes to firm up and remove as much moisture as possible (see page 194 for photo). Cut the tofu into ½-inch slabs and pat thoroughly dry.

2. In a small bowl, whisk together the orange juice, brown sugar, garlic, ginger, soy sauce, gochujang, sesame oil, lime zest and juice. Set aside.

3. In a large nonstick skillet over medium-high heat, heat the canola oil. When the oil is hot and rippling across the surface, carefully add the tofu. Cook for 5 minutes, or until very crisp and dark brown underneath. Carefully flip the tofu and cook for another 5 minutes, until crisp and dark brown on the other side. Remove the tofu from the skillet and pour the oil into a small bowl (discard when cool). Return the skillet to medium heat and add the sauce mixture. Bring the sauce to a simmer, return the tofu to the skillet, and cook for 5 minutes, basting the tofu occasionally, or until the glaze is thick enough to coat a spoon.

4. To serve, divide the tofu and rice among the lettuce cups. Drizzle with the glaze and top with chives, chiles, and sesame seeds. Serve with lime wedges.

Note

Gochujang is a fermented Korean chili paste that is available in Asian markets, some grocery stores, and on Amazon. I love the Koko Kosher Korean brand, but it's also available from O'Food. If you can't find it, use a teaspoon of sriracha mixed with a bit of miso paste instead.

Chickpea Curry

Serves 6

My pantry is packed with a variety of canned beans for quick and easy dinners. I use pinto beans for refried bean tacos, black beans for chili, and cannellini beans for soups. Chickpeas are a staple for quick and easy hummus, tagines, and curries. This saucy curry dinner comes together in no time and makes a hearty, cozy meal on a cold winter night.

2 tablespoons extra-virgin olive oil

1 medium red onion, diced small

1 tablespoon finely minced fresh ginger

2 garlic cloves, minced

1 tablespoon Garam Masala (page 304 or store-bought)

1 tablespoon curry powder

3 (15.5-ounce) cans chickpeas, rinsed and drained

1 (14-ounce) can diced tomatoes and juices

1 (14-ounce) can full-fat coconut milk

Kosher salt and freshly ground black pepper to taste

Brown rice, basmati rice, couscous, or quinoa, for serving

Chopped scallions and fresh cilantro leaves, for garnish

Lime wedges and yogurt, for serving (optional)

1. In a large skillet over medium heat, heat the olive oil. Add the onion, ginger, and garlic and sauté for 5 minutes, or until the mixture is soft and fragrant but not browned. Add the garam masala and curry powder and sauté for 1 minute, or until fragrant.

2. Stir in the chickpeas, tomatoes and their juices, and coconut milk. Bring the mixture to a simmer and season with salt and pepper. Cover the pot and simmer for 25 to 30 minutes, until the sauce is thickened.

3. To serve, spoon the curry over the starch of your choice. Garnish with scallions and cilantro and finish with a squeeze of lime juice and dollop of yogurt, if desired.

Variation

You can also serve this in a grain bowl with roasted squash (season butternut or kabocha squash with a few pinches of garam masala, a drizzle of olive oil, honey, and salt, and roast at 400°F for 25 minutes, or until tender), quinoa, or sautéed kale.

Freezer-Friendly

To freeze the curry, transfer to an airtight container and freeze for up to 2 months.

Smashed Falafel

Makes 20 patties

You know when you come up with an awesome idea and you're like, why didn't anyone else think of it? Well, you're lookin' at her! I was frying up falafel one jolly Meatless Monday when I asked myself; If the crunchy shell of falafel is the best part, why doesn't anyone flatten it for more surface area? And it hit me—Smashed Falafel à la smash burgers, only SO MUCH CRISPIER! You're welcome!

1 pound dried chickpeas
1 cup packed fresh parsley leaves
1 cup packed fresh cilantro leaves
1 large Spanish onion, roughly chopped
5 garlic cloves
1 cup all-purpose flour
1 tablespoon ground coriander
1 tablespoon ground cumin
1 tablespoon kosher salt
½ teaspoon baking soda
1 extra-large egg white
Canola oil, for frying
Extra-Creamy Tahini (page 301), Jeweled Hummus (page 50), Schug (page 301), Smoky Harissa (page 303), and/or Israeli salad (see page 56), for serving

1. In a large bowl, combine the chickpeas with enough water to cover by 3 to 4 inches and set aside at room temperature overnight or for at least 12 hours. Rinse the chickpeas and drain well.

2. In a food processor fitted with the S blade, pulse the chickpeas until the mixture is piecey but not finely ground. You want some smaller and some larger bits. Transfer to a large bowl.

3. In the food processor fitted with the S blade, pulse the parsley, cilantro, onion, and garlic until finely chopped, then add the mixture to the bowl with the chickpeas.

4. To the chickpea mixture, add the flour, coriander, cumin, salt, baking soda, and egg white and stir until the ingredients are fully combined.

5. In a cast-iron skillet or heavy-bottomed frying pan over medium-high heat, heat ½ cup oil. Add ¼ cup chickpea batter to the pan and flatten with a spatula so it's ¼ inch thick. Repeat with two more portions of falafel batter, or however many you can fit in the skillet without overcrowding. Fry for 5 minutes, or until crisp and golden on the bottom. Flip the patty and fry the second side another 5 minutes, until crisp and golden. Drain on a paper towel–lined plate or baking sheet and immediately transfer to a rack so it remains crisp. Repeat with the remaining batter, adding more oil as needed.

6. Serve in a pita or burger bun or over a salad with Extra-Creamy Tahini and toppings of your choice.

Freezer-Friendly

Tempeh Shawarma

Serves 6

Unlike tofu, which is made from curdled soy milk pressed into blocks, tempeh is made from cooked fermented soybeans, which are pressed to form a patty. Tempeh has a dense, chewy texture and an earthy, nutty flavor, which lends itself well to any marinade. One Sukkot, I was hosting my sister-in-law's family, and her dad is a vegetarian. I threw together this shawarma for him last minute, and he couldn't get enough! You can serve the tempeh in a pita or laffa or over freekeh, farro, or couscous as a bowl.

2 (8-ounce) packages tempeh (see Note)

6 tablespoons extra-virgin olive oil, divided

3 tablespoons Shawarma Spice (page 304)

1 large Spanish onion, thinly sliced into half-moons

Kosher salt to taste

Jeweled Hummus (page 50), Extra-Creamy Tahini (page 301), Schug (page 301), Smoky Harissa (page 303), Israeli salad (see page 56), cabbage salad (see page 98), roasted chickpeas (see page 62), labneh, and/or yogurt, for serving (optional)

1. Cut the tempeh in half lengthwise through the middle so you have two thin, long rectangles from each package. Stack the pieces of tempeh on top of each other and slice crosswise thinly (about ⅛ inch) into shards so it resembles sliced shawarma. In a large bowl, mix the tempeh with 4 tablespoons of the olive oil and the Shawarma Spice and set aside to marinate for at least 1 hour or up to overnight.

2. In a large skillet over medium heat, heat the remaining 2 tablespoons olive oil. Add the onion and sauté for 25 minutes, until deeply browned. Add the tempeh to the pan and continue to sauté for 10 more minutes, stirring occasionally, or until the tempeh crisps up.

3. Serve in a bowl with grains, or with bread, and toppings of your choice.

Note

Some people find tempeh to be bitter. To remove some of the bitterness, you can steam the tempeh in a steamer basket or pasta strainer set into a shallow amount of boiling water. Cover the pot and steam for 10 minutes prior to using.

Variation

Use quartered cremini or white button mushrooms instead of tempeh.

Enoki Pulled "Beef"

Serves 2 to 4

Enoki mushrooms are the cutest little noodle-like mushrooms that grow in tight bunches. You may have seen them nestled in ramen soup. I've discovered that they actually mimic pulled beef incredibly well. Instead of washing mushrooms in water (they soak it up like a sponge, which prevents caramelization), use a pastry brush or paper towels to carefully clean away any dirt.

14 ounces enoki mushrooms, ends trimmed, pulled apart into small sections

3 tablespoons extra-virgin olive oil

2 tablespoons (packed) dark brown sugar

2 teaspoons smoked paprika

2 teaspoons garlic powder

½ teaspoon mustard powder

½ teaspoon kosher salt

¼ teaspoon freshly ground black pepper

¼ cup barbecue sauce

1. Preheat the oven to 400°F. Line a baking sheet with parchment paper.

2. Spread the mushrooms on the baking sheet. Drizzle the olive oil over the mushrooms and add the brown sugar, paprika, garlic powder, mustard powder, salt, and pepper, tossing to evenly coat the mushrooms in the spices. Roast for 35 minutes, stirring occasionally, until the mushrooms are caramelized around the edges.

3. Remove the mushrooms from the oven and stir in the barbecue sauce. Serve warm.

4. Serve in tortillas, on a bun for pulled beef sliders, stuffed into eggrolls, over nachos, stirred into pasta, or over rice.

All-Purpose Pizza Dough
Makes 24 ounces dough

Let's face it, we all reach for that ball of all-purpose pizza dough from the freezer section at the grocery store when we're in a pinch. But making your own is easier than you think, and it comes together in no time! Use it to make khachapuri (see page 208), garlic knots (see page 49), or homemade pizza for dairy night.

1 tablespoon active dry yeast
1 teaspoon sugar
1 cup warm water
2½ cups all-purpose flour, plus
   2 to 4 tablespoons, as needed
2 tablespoons extra-virgin olive oil
1 teaspoon kosher salt

1. In a large bowl, combine the yeast, sugar, and warm water and let it rest for 5 minutes, or until foamy.

2. Add the flour, olive oil, and salt and mix with a spoon for 1 minute, or until a mildly sticky dough forms. Add more flour, a tablespoon at a time, and knead with your hands to incorporate the flour until the dough doesn't stick to your fingers. Cover the bowl with a kitchen towel and place in a warm spot to rise for 1 hour, or until doubled in size.

3. Roll the dough out with a rolling pin or stretch it out with your fingers. Top with your favorite pizza toppings, or divide into portions for homemade calzones, savory babka, garlic knots, or breadsticks.

Freezer-Friendly
You can freeze the dough before or after shaping. Thaw the dough in the refrigerator, rise at room temperature for 20 minutes, then shape and bake.

Spinach Artichoke Khachapuri
Serves 8

I first tried khachapuri at a restaurant called Khachapuria in the Machane Yehuda Shuk in Jerusalem. The dish, made with a cheesy filling topped with an egg yolk, is named after the boat-shaped breads that are native to Georgia. It was one of the best foods I had ever tried, and when I returned home, I was euphoric to find that Marani, a kosher Georgian restaurant in Queens, had a meaty version that was equally delicious. This adaptation was inspired by the classic spinach artichoke dip, which pairs wonderfully with the runny egg yolk.

1 cup ricotta or whipped cottage cheese
1 cup (packed) shredded mozzarella
½ cup crumbled feta
¼ cup grated Parmesan
1 (10-ounce) package frozen spinach, thawed, drained, and squeezed dry
1 (14-ounce) can artichokes, drained and chopped
2 garlic cloves, minced
Freshly ground black pepper to taste
1 recipe All-Purpose Pizza Dough (page 207)
2 tablespoons extra-virgin olive oil
2 extra-large egg yolks
2 tablespoons unsalted butter

1. Place two sheet trays in the oven and preheat to 425°F.

2. In a large bowl, combine the ricotta, mozzarella, feta, and Parmesan. Mix in the spinach, artichokes, and garlic. Season with pepper.

3. Divide the pizza dough in half. On two lightly floured sheets of parchment paper, use a rolling pin to roll out each piece of dough into a rough oval shape (about 10 × 15 inches). Divide and spoon the cheese mixture evenly into the center of each dough, leaving a 2-inch border. Roll the edges over so that the dough wraps around the cheese to form a "boat," twisting the ends closed.

4. Using oven mitts, carefully remove the sheet trays from the oven and transfer the boats by carefully lifting both sides of the parchment paper onto the trays. Brush the exposed dough with olive oil. Bake the khachapuri for 20 minutes, until the crust is golden and the cheese is melting. Remove from the oven and use a spoon to make a well in the center of the cheese mixture. Place a yolk into the well of each khachapuri. Return to the oven and bake for 3 minutes, or until the yolks are just set around the edges but still runny. Transfer the khachapuri to a serving platter.

5. Dot each khachapuri with 1 tablespoon of the butter. To eat, stir the eggs and butter into the hot cheese. Tear off pieces of the dough from the edges and dip them into the cheese and egg mixture.

Leek and Corn Crustless Ricotta Quiche

Serves 8

Because I'm such a texture girl, the custardy mouthfeel of quiche has never really been my thing, so I decided to play around with fillings to give it a little something extra. The ricotta almost transforms this dish into a savory cheesecake, and the sweet little nuggets of corn give it a welcome pop. I've been converted!

1 tablespoon unsalted butter, plus more for greasing the pan

8 ounces shredded Muenster cheese

1 tablespoon extra-virgin olive oil

1 large leek, washed and chopped

Kosher salt to taste

1 (15.25-ounce) can corn, drained, or 1½ cups thawed frozen corn

2 garlic cloves, minced

Freshly ground black pepper to taste

5 extra-large eggs

½ cup whole or low-fat milk

1 cup ricotta cheese

1. Preheat the oven to 350°F.

2. Grease a 10-inch deep pie dish with butter and spread half of the Muenster cheese on the bottom of the dish. Set aside.

3. In a large skillet over medium heat, heat 1 tablespoon butter and the olive oil. Add the chopped leek, season with salt, and sauté for 15 minutes, or until caramelized. Add the corn and garlic and continue to sauté for 3 minutes, or until fragrant. Season with salt and pepper and set aside.

4. In a large bowl, whisk together the eggs and milk. Add the ricotta and mix with a spoon until well combined. Season with salt and pepper.

5. Spread the sautéed vegetables over the cheese on the bottom of the pie dish. Pour the ricotta mixture over the vegetables and top with the remaining Muenster cheese.

6. Transfer the pie dish to the oven and bake for 30 to 35 minutes, until the quiche is just set and the cheese is bubbly and starting to brown.

Variation

Feel free to experiment with different vegetables of your choice.

Mushroom Ftut for Two

Serves 2

When I was in my teens, my friend Dina and I would frequent an Israeli café named Bissaleh, talking over malawach (a Yemenite flatbread with flaky, crispy layers), bourekas, and sachlav until the wee hours of the morning. When we needed comfort food, we'd order ftut, which was essentially a malawach-based matzo Brei mixed with cheese and other fill-ins. Bissaleh did not last, but Dina is still one of my closest friends, and the mushroom was her favorite. Dina, this one's for you!

1 tablespoon extra-virgin olive oil

6 ounces button mushrooms, stemmed and sliced

2 tablespoons unsalted butter

2 discs frozen malawach dough, thawed

3 extra-large eggs

1 cup shredded mozzarella

Kosher salt and freshly ground black pepper to taste

Resek (page 301) and Schug (page 301), for dipping

1. In a large skillet over medium-high heat, heat the olive oil. Add the mushrooms and sauté for 5 minutes, or until the liquid evaporates and the mushrooms start to caramelize. Transfer the mushrooms to a plate and set aside.

2. Place the butter in the skillet and fry the malawach dough 3 minutes per side, or until browned and crisp. Transfer the malawach to a cutting board and chop it into 1-inch pieces. In a large bowl, combine the chopped malawach with the eggs, mozzarella, mushrooms, salt, and pepper.

3. Pour the mixture back into the skillet and cook over medium-high heat for approximately 3 minutes, stirring every minute or so, or until the eggs are set and the cheese is melted.

4. Serve immediately with Resek and Schug.

Variation

Try the ftut with different fill-ins such as olives, sautéed onions, or roasted eggplant. You can also top with feta or za'atar, if desired.

Pumpkin Gnocchi Alfredo
Serves 4

I'm not much of a pumpkin spice gal. I'd choose gingersnap over pumpkin spice any day (see my Hawaij Gingersnaps on page 254). But a savory pumpkin sauce is something I can get behind. Here, I elevate a simple Alfredo cream sauce by adding pumpkin, chestnuts, and sage to coat the gnocchi in a rich and decadent sauce that's worth the effort.

4 tablespoons unsalted butter, divided

5 whole sage leaves, for garnish

1 (16-ounce) package store-bought gnocchi

3 garlic cloves, minced

1 shallot, minced

3½ ounces roasted chestnuts, roughly chopped

1 tablespoon chopped fresh sage (about 5 leaves)

1 cup canned pumpkin purée (not pumpkin pie filling)

1½ cups heavy cream

¼ teaspoon ground nutmeg

1 teaspoon kosher salt

¼ teaspoon freshly ground black pepper

⅓ cup grated Parmesan, plus more for serving

1. In a large skillet over medium heat, melt 2 tablespoons of the butter. Add 5 whole sage leaves (or however many you'd like!) and fry for 1 minute, or until crispy. Use a slotted spoon or tongs to transfer the fried sage to a paper towel–lined plate and set aside to use as a garnish.

2. Add the gnocchi to the pan and cook over medium heat for 5 to 8 minutes, until softened and starting to brown and crisp. Remove the gnocchi from the skillet and transfer to a plate.

3. Place the remaining 2 tablespoons butter in the skillet. Add the garlic, shallot, and chestnuts. Cook over medium heat, stirring, for 3 minutes, or until softened and fragrant but not browned. Add the chopped sage and nutmeg and stir for 1 minute, until fragrant. Add the pumpkin purée, heavy cream, nutmeg, salt, and pepper and stir until incorporated. Stir in the Parmesan cheese and simmer for 3 minutes, or until thickened. If the mixture is too thick, add a bit of water or cream to thin it out to desired consistency; the sauce should be creamy.

4. Stir in the gnocchi and simmer for 3 more minutes. Garnish with the fried sage and serve immediately with more Parmesan.

Variation

Toss the sauce with fettuccine instead of gnocchi for an autumn spin on fettuccine Alfredo.

Sweet Noodle Kugel Latkes with Bourbon Raisin Jam

Serves 8

Sweet noodle kugel batter fried into crispy bites of deliciousness is the best of kugel and latkes combined for a perfect brunch or Chanukah treat! Since not everyone likes raisins, I took them out and created a flavor bomb of raisin jam that will make you see raisins in a whole new light. If you're a raisin fan (and even if you're not!), you're going to want to add it to your next cheese board, slather it on your morning toast, and eat it by the spoonful.

12 ounces medium egg noodles (not curly)
4 extra-large eggs
16 ounces ricotta or whipped cottage cheese
¾ cup all-purpose flour
⅔ cup sugar
1 teaspoon ground cinnamon
1 teaspoon pure vanilla extract
½ teaspoon kosher salt
1 stick (8 tablespoons) unsalted butter, for frying
Sour cream, for serving

BOURBON RAISIN JAM
1 cup dark raisins
¾ cup apple cider
½ cup bourbon
Juice of 1 lemon
1 cinnamon stick
Pinch of kosher salt

1. Bring a medium pot of salted water to a boil and add the egg noodles. Cook for 7 to 8 minutes, until al dente, and drain well.

2. While the noodles are cooking, make the jam: In a small saucepan, combine the raisins, apple cider, bourbon, lemon juice, cinnamon stick, and salt and bring the mixture to a simmer over medium heat. Cook for 10 to 15 minutes, until the liquid is reduced and thickened. Transfer the jam to a food processor fitted with the S blade or blender and pulse until the desired consistency is reached (I prefer it on the chunky side). Set aside.

3. In a large bowl, combine the eggs, ricotta, flour, sugar, cinnamon, vanilla, and salt and stir until creamy. Add in the pasta and mix until incorporated.

4. In a large nonstick frying pan over medium heat, melt the butter. Using a ¼-cup measure or ice cream scoop, portion out the noodle mixture and fry 5 minutes per side, or until golden brown on both sides.

5. Serve with sour cream and the jam.

Shakshuka à la Lasagne

Serves 2 to 4

I have never met a shakshuka I didn't like, and I have experimented with many! From ramen shakshuka to shakshuka made with roasted eggplant, spaghetti squash, and zoodles, I'm always having fun with different combinations. This shakshuka doesn't have actual noodles in it, but the sauce and cheese have #allthefeels of the layered pasta dish.

2 tablespoons extra-virgin olive oil

2 garlic cloves, minced

2 tablespoons tomato paste

½ cup thawed and squeezed-dry chopped frozen spinach

1 (16-ounce) can tomato sauce

½ tablespoon honey

Kosher salt and freshly ground black pepper to taste

½ cup ricotta or whipped cottage cheese

1 tablespoon grated Parmesan, plus 2 tablespoons for topping

¼ teaspoon dried basil

¼ teaspoon dried oregano

5 extra-large eggs

½ cup shredded mozzarella cheese

Fresh basil, chopped, for garnish

Crusty bread, for serving

1. In a large oven-safe skillet over medium heat, heat the olive oil. Add the garlic and sauté for 2 minutes, or until fragrant but not browned. Add the tomato paste and cook for 3 minutes, stirring until darkened. Add the spinach, tomato sauce, honey, salt, and pepper and bring the mixture to a simmer.

2. In a small bowl, combine the ricotta, 1 tablespoon of the Parmesan, basil, oregano, and pepper.

3. Make five wells in the sauce and crack an egg into each one. Place 2-tablespoon dollops of the ricotta mixture around the pan and sprinkle the mozzarella over the top. Cover the pan with foil and cook for 3 minutes, or until the eggs are mostly set. In the meantime, preheat your oven to broil.

4. Sprinkle the shakshuka with the remaining 2 tablespoons Parmesan and transfer to the oven with the rack in the highest position. Broil for 1 to 2 minutes, until the cheese is bubbling and starting to brown.

5. Garnish with the fresh basil and eat immediately with crusty bread.

Veg & Sides

Curried Cauliflower
Serves 4 to 6

I never met a cauliflower recipe I didn't like. Sometimes I even nosh on the florets raw—they're crunchy like chips but way better for you! Roasting brings out cauliflower's natural sweetness, so I love a good caramelized char on them too. This dish is as flavorful as it is pretty!

¼ cup extra-virgin olive oil

1 tablespoon honey

1 teaspoon curry powder

1 teaspoon ground turmeric

¼ teaspoon ground ginger

1 large cauliflower, whole

Kosher salt and freshly ground black pepper to taste

⅓ cup pine nuts, for garnish

¼ cup raw tahini paste, for garnish

½ cup golden raisins, for garnish

Fresh mint, for garnish

1. Preheat the oven to 425°F. Line a baking sheet with parchment paper.

2. In a small bowl, combine the olive oil, honey, curry powder, turmeric, and ginger. Place the cauliflower on the baking sheet or in the shallow pan. Brush the cauliflower with the seasoning mix and sprinkle generously with salt and pepper. Roast for 35 to 40 minutes, until the cauliflower is tender and caramelized. Remove from the oven.

3. Reduce the oven temperature to 350°F. Place the pine nuts on a small baking sheet and bake for 8 minutes, until lightly toasted.

4. Transfer the roasted cauliflower to a serving dish and garnish with tahini, pine nuts, raisins, and mint.

Notes

- *This preparation will yield a tender-crisp cauliflower. For a softer interior, bring a pot of salted water to a boil and blanch the cauliflower for 6 minutes, or until it is pierced easily with a knife. Dry well, then continue as above.*

- *To roast the cauliflower in florets, spread the florets out on a parchment-lined baking sheet, toss with the olive oil, honey, curry powder, turmeric, ginger, salt, and pepper and roast for 25 minutes.*

Party-in-Your-Mouth Peppers

Serves 6 to 8

If you're like me, you always walk past the bag of mini multicolored peppers in the supermarket wondering what to do with them. They're so bright and vibrant, but… what do you *do* with them? Well, here you go: first you roast them so they become sweet like candy, and then you smother them in briny olives, tangy vinegar, and fruity olive oil for a full-on party in your mouth.

2 pounds mini sweet peppers, sliced in half, seeds, veins, and stems removed

6 tablespoons extra-virgin olive oil, divided

Kosher salt and freshly ground black pepper to taste

2 garlic cloves, minced

2 tablespoons minced shallots

3 tablespoons red wine vinegar

3 tablespoons minced kalamata olives

¼ cup chopped fresh parsley, for garnish

Maldon sea salt flakes, for garnish (optional)

1. Preheat the oven to 425°F. Line a baking sheet with parchment paper.

2. To roast the peppers, spread them out, cut-side down, on the prepared baking sheet and drizzle with 2 tablespoons of the olive oil. Season with salt and pepper, toss to coat, and bake for 25 minutes, until the peppers are tender and blistered in spots.

3. Meanwhile, in a small bowl, whisk together the garlic, shallots, olives, remaining 4 tablespoons olive oil, and vinegar.

4. Spread the roasted peppers on a serving tray. Drizzle with the dressing and garnish with parsley, and Maldon sea salt, if desired.

Everything Green Beans

Serves 6

Is there anything that doesn't benefit from a happy sprinkle of everything bagel spice? In my house, we put it on *everything* from eggs to salads, grilled chicken to challah, grilled cheese, popcorn, and even fries! If you're looking for a healthy veggie to snack on or an easy vegetable side that everyone will go for, these beans are addictive and deeelish—try them!

1½ pounds green beans, ends trimmed
3 tablespoons extra-virgin olive oil
¼ cup Everything Bagel Spice (page 305)
Kosher salt to taste

1. Preheat the oven to 425°F. Line a baking sheet with parchment paper.

2. Spread the green beans on the baking sheet and coat with the olive oil. Sprinkle with the Everything Bagel Spice and season with salt. Toss to evenly coat the green beans and roast for 25 minutes, tossing halfway through, until tender-crisp.

Roasted Tzimmes Purée with Date Gremolata
Serves 6 to 8

Say goodbye to the cloyingly sweet, prune-dimpled tzimmes of yesteryear, and say hello to this bright, creamy, and sophisticated purée with the same flavors of carrot and orange that will transport you to the original, only it's creamier, healthier, and infinitely more delicious.

2 pounds butternut squash

3 large carrots, peeled, cut in chunks

3 tablespoons extra-virgin olive oil

Kosher salt and freshly ground black pepper to taste

1 tablespoon honey

Juice of 1 orange (reserve zest for gremolata)

½ cup canned full-fat coconut milk

DATE GREMOLATA

2 tablespoons finely minced shallot

3 tablespoons finely chopped fresh parsley

2 medjool dates, pitted, diced small

1 tablespoon orange zest

3 tablespoons extra-virgin olive oil

Kosher salt and freshly ground black pepper to taste

1. Preheat the oven to 400°F. Line a baking sheet with parchment paper.

2. Cut the butternut squash in half lengthwise and remove the seeds (do not peel). Place it, cut-side down, on the baking sheet. Add the carrot chunks and drizzle with olive oil. Season with salt and pepper. Roast for 1 hour, or until the vegetables are fork-tender.

3. While the vegetables are roasting, prepare the gremolata: In a small bowl, combine the shallot, parsley, dates, reserved orange zest, and olive oil and toss. Season with salt and pepper.

4. Scoop the flesh out of the butternut squash and add to a food processor with the S blade attached. Add the roasted carrots, honey, orange juice, and coconut milk and blend until smooth and creamy. Depending on your machine, this make take a few minutes.

5. Serve the tzimmes purée warm with the gremolata on top.

Variation

Use dried figs, prunes, or apricots (or a combination!) in the gremolata instead of the dates.

Freezer-Friendly

(purée only)

Roasted Eggplant with Harissa-Braised Chickpeas

Serves 8

People often ask me if all of my kids eat my food, and the answer is no. I wish I could say I am the fairy godmother of children's meals, but the truth is, I've got picky eaters just like everyone else. Case in point: I often tease one of my picky eaters that everything on her plate is brown (she's not a fan of fruits or vegetables). She happens to love chickpeas, so I started preparing a braised version with a spicy harissa sauce that I serve every Shabbat. Now her plate has red on it, and since there's tomato sauce in it, we like to say she's eating a vegetable!

2 tablespoons extra-virgin olive oil

2 tablespoons Smoky Harissa (page 303 or store-bought), or to taste

3 tablespoons tomato paste

3 garlic cloves, minced

2 (15-ounce) cans chickpeas, rinsed and drained

½ bunch of cilantro, leaves and stems roughly chopped (reserve some leaves for garnish)

Juice and zest of 1 lemon

1 to 2 tablespoons honey

2 teaspoons kosher salt

EGGPLANT

2 large eggplants

2 tablespoons grapeseed oil

Kosher salt to taste

Juice of 1 lemon

Extra-Creamy Tahini (page 301), for serving

1. In a 10-inch sauté pan over medium heat, heat the olive oil. Add the harissa and tomato paste and sauté for 4 minutes, until the paste is dark and caramelized. Add the garlic and stir for 1 minute, or until fragrant. Add the chickpeas, cilantro, lemon zest, lemon juice, honey, 2½ cups water, and the salt. Cover the pot, leaving the lid slightly ajar, bring to a boil, then reduce to a simmer and cook over low heat for 1 hour, or until the chickpeas are very soft and the sauce has thickened. Adjust the seasoning by adding more harissa, honey, lemon, or salt to taste.

2. Preheat the oven to high broil with the oven rack in the highest position. Place the eggplants on a baking sheet and brush with grapeseed oil on all sides. Poke the eggplants with a fork a few times. Broil the eggplant for 25 minutes, turning every 5 minutes or so, or until the skin is charred all over and the flesh is soft.

3. To serve, cool the eggplant slightly and gently remove and discard the charred skin (it's okay if some of it stays on), leaving the stem intact. Transfer the eggplant to a serving platter and spread the flesh out, seasoning it with salt and lemon juice. Top the eggplant with the Extra-Creamy Tahini and braised chickpeas and garnish with cilantro leaves.

Note

You can adjust the sweetness depending on the spiciness of the harissa.

Japanese Sweet Potatoes with Miso Tahini Butter

Serves 8

Because they're a little drier and starchier than other varieties, Japanese sweet potatoes have a distinct creaminess and a fluffier, lighter texture that is like a cross between a russet potato and a sweet potato. Its nutty flavor pairs well with sweet and savory applications, and instead of roasting them whole, I halve them and roast them, cut-side down, which cuts back considerably on cooking time and forms a crispy caramelized crust (thanks to Kim Kushner for this magical technique). This sweet, spicy, and smoky coating makes the potatoes extra addictive!

¼ cup grapeseed oil

1 tablespoon (packed) dark brown sugar

2 tablespoons maple syrup

2 teaspoons smoked paprika

1 teaspoon chili powder

1 teaspoon kosher salt

¼ teaspoon ground cinnamon

Pinch of cayenne pepper

4 Japanese sweet potatoes, scrubbed and halved lengthwise

MISO TAHINI BUTTER

3 tablespoons tahini paste

1 tablespoon white (shiro) miso paste

2 teaspoons maple syrup

1. Preheat the oven to 400°F. Line a baking sheet with parchment paper.

2. In a small bowl, combine the grapeseed oil, brown sugar, maple syrup, paprika, chili powder, salt, cinnamon, and cayenne pepper.

3. Transfer the sweet potato halves to the prepared baking sheet and brush both sides with the seasoned oil. Roast, cut-side down on the bottom oven rack, for 30 to 40 minutes, until the potatoes are caramelized and easily pierced with a fork.

4. To prepare the miso tahini butter, combine the tahini paste with the miso, maple syrup, and 1 tablespoon of water in a small bowl and whisk until creamy. Serve with sweet potatoes.

Za'atar Smashed Brussels Sprouts

Serves 4 to 6

Brussels sprouts have always presented a problem in the kosher kitchen because the leaves are tightly packed and they are often infested with worms. When greenhouse-grown frozen Brussels sprouts became available on the kosher market, I was thrilled, but getting the frozen nuggets to crisp up proved challenging. Alas, I discovered the perfect method to achieve crispy, previously frozen cruciferous perfection—smashing the thawed sprouts so that they are thinner and have more surface area, then roasting them at a high cooking temperature on the bottom oven rack for ultimate caramelization. I tell you, this is Brussels sprouts gold!

1 (16-ounce) package frozen Brussels sprouts, thawed
2 tablespoons extra-virgin olive oil
1½ tablespoons za'atar
1 tablespoon silan (date honey)
Kosher salt to taste
Crumbled feta, for garnish (optional)
Pomegranate seeds, for garnish (optional)

1. Preheat the oven to 450°F and adjust an oven rack to the bottom position. Line a baking sheet with parchment paper.

2. Remove the Brussels sprouts from the package and use a kitchen towel to pat them dry, removing as much moisture as possible. Spread the Brussels sprouts on the prepared baking sheet.

3. Using a dry measuring cup or drinking glass, place the cup on top of each sprout and use your hand to press down and flatten the sprout as flat as you can. Pat the sprouts dry again. Drizzle with olive oil and season with za'atar, silan, and salt. Toss to coat evenly.

4. Bake on the bottom rack of the oven for 20 to 25 minutes, until the Brussels sprouts are crispy and caramelized. Serve warm or at room temperature.

5. For dairy meals, top with feta and pomegranate seeds.

Orange Cardamom Rice

Serves 8

This fragrant and festive baked rice makes a beautiful bed for pulled beef (Slow Cooker Berbere Brisket, page 188), roast turkey (Turkey Roast with Za'atar Gravy, page 172), or grilled chicken (Lemon Sumac Grilled Chicken Thighs, page 163). Festive enough for holiday meals, yet simple enough for every day. Win-win!

¼ cup extra-virgin olive oil

1 large Spanish onion, finely diced

2 large carrots, grated

1 teaspoon ground cardamom

Zest and juice of 1 medium orange

2 cups basmati rice

2 teaspoons kosher salt

1 teaspoon freshly ground black pepper

1. Preheat the oven to 350°F.

2. In a large skillet over medium heat, heat the oil. Add the onions and carrots and sauté for 6 minutes, or until softened. Add the cardamom and orange zest and sauté for 1 minute, or until fragrant. Stir in the rice and sauté for 3 minutes, until coated in oil and slightly toasted.

3. Pour the rice into a 9 × 13-inch baking dish. Add 3 cups water, ½ cup orange juice, the salt, and pepper and stir. Cover the baking dish with parchment paper and a layer of foil. Transfer to the preheated oven and bake for 1 hour, until the liquid is absorbed and the rice is cooked through. Fluff with a fork and serve warm.

Note

If your orange yields less than ½ cup juice, add water to make up the difference.

Herbed Farro Pilaf

Serves 8

I can't get enough of farro's nutty flavor and chewy bite. It's such a lovely
and healthy grain! This herb-forward green pilaf was inspired by bachsh,
the Bukharian green rice pilaf that is sometimes studded with meat or
chicken. This vegan version complements any protein as a colorful, flavorful,
and delicious dish—or use it as a base for a hearty grain bowl.

1 cup fresh parsley leaves

1 cup fresh cilantro leaves

1 cup baby spinach

½ cup fresh dill fronds

3 scallions (white and green parts), roughly chopped

1 leek (white and pale green parts only), washed and roughly chopped

3 tablespoons extra-virgin olive oil

16 ounces Italian pearled farro, rinsed and drained

4 cups vegetable stock

2 teaspoons kosher salt

½ teaspoon freshly ground black pepper

1. In the bowl of a food processor fitted with the S blade, combine the parsley, cilantro, spinach, dill, scallions, and leek. Pulse until finely chopped.

2. In a 6-quart pot over medium heat, heat the olive oil. Add the chopped herbs and sauté for 5 minutes, until wilted. Add the farro and continue to sauté for an additional 5 minutes, until the farro is coated and the mixture is fragrant. Add the stock, salt, and pepper and bring to a boil. Reduce the heat to low and simmer, uncovered, for 25 minutes, stirring occasionally, until the liquid is absorbed. Remove the farro from the heat, cover with a lid, and steam for 10 minutes, until the farro is tender.

The
Bakery

Baklava Palmiers

Makes 40 cookies

Baklava is a labor-intensive dessert, especially considering the layers of phyllo pastry that tear and dry out easily. So I took the same ingredients and turned them into baklava-inspired palmiers! Also known as elephant ears, these cute crisps puff up beautifully in the oven and come together in no time.

2 sheets frozen puff pastry, thawed (Pepperidge Farm recommended)
5 ounces finely chopped walnuts (about 1 cup)
½ cup (firmly packed) dark brown sugar
½ teaspoon ground cinnamon
¼ teaspoon kosher salt
¼ cup honey (optional)

1. Preheat the oven to 400°F. Line two baking sheets with parchment paper.

2. Remove the puff pastry from the package and unfold each sheet. Roll out lightly to smooth out the folds.

3. In a small bowl, stir together the walnuts, brown sugar, cinnamon, and salt.

4. Sprinkle half of the walnut mixture onto one of the puff pastry sheets and press down with a rolling pin to adhere the filling to the dough. Fold the left and right sides of the pastry toward the center so they go halfway to the middle. Fold them again so the two folds meet exactly at the middle of the dough. Then fold one half over the other half as though closing a book. You will have six layers. Freeze the dough for 20 minutes.

5. Slice the dough crosswise into ⅜-inch slices and place the slices, cut-side up, on the baking sheets. Repeat with the second sheet of pastry and the remaining nut filling.

6. Bake the palmiers for 18 minutes, until browned and caramelized on the bottom. Transfer them to a baking rack to cool.

7. If desired, in a small saucepan, combine the honey with ¼ cup water. Bring it to a simmer over low heat and cook for 5 minutes. Brush the honey syrup over the warm cookies with a pastry brush. (This will soften the cookies, so if you prefer them crispy, skip this step.)

8. To store the cookies, skip the honey glaze and transfer the palmiers to a zip-top bag. Store at room temperature for up to 3 days or freeze for up to 2 months.

Freezer-Friendly

Harvest Bundt Cake

Serves 12

I love the simplicity and beauty of an elegant, iced Bundt cake—especially the way the icing falls down the sides. Decorating the cake with the best of the harvest season, using apples, figs, and pomegranates, makes this a stunning holiday centerpiece. And with apples and honey, it's perfect for Rosh Hashanah.

3 extra-large eggs

1 cup (packed) dark brown sugar

1 cup canola oil

1 cup honey

3 cups all-purpose flour, plus more for flouring the pan

1½ teaspoons baking powder

1½ teaspoons baking soda

1 teaspoon plus ⅛ teaspoon ground cinnamon, divided

½ teaspoon ground ginger

¼ teaspoon ground nutmeg

½ teaspoon kosher salt

1 cup plus 2 tablespoons apple cider, divided

2 Granny Smith apples, peeled, cored, and grated

1½ cups confectioners sugar

For decorating: Cinnamon sticks; star anise; fresh figs, halved; gooseberries; pomegranate seeds; baby apples; honeycomb

1. Preheat the oven to 350°F. Grease a nonstick Bundt pan with cooking spray and lightly flour it.

2. In a large bowl using an electric mixer, beat the eggs and brown sugar until creamy. Add the oil and honey and beat until fully combined.

3. In a separate medium bowl, whisk together the flour, baking powder, baking soda, 1 teaspoon of the cinnamon, the ginger, nutmeg, and salt.

4. Add the dry ingredients into the bowl with the wet ingredients and mix well. Add 1 cup of the apple cider and the grated apples and stir until combined.

5. Pour the batter into the Bundt pan and bake for 50 minutes, until a toothpick inserted comes out clean. Cool for 10 minutes, then run a knife around the edges to loosen the cake from the pan. Unmold onto a cake stand and cool completely.

6. To prepare the icing, in a small bowl, whisk together the confectioners sugar, the remaining 2 tablespoons apple cider, and the remaining ⅛ teaspoon cinnamon until smooth. Pour the icing over the cake so that it drips down the sides.

7. While the icing is still tacky, decorate the cake with the toppings of your choice. Serve immediately.

8. This cake gets better as it sits but is best eaten within a few days. Remove the toppings from leftover cake so it doesn't get soggy.

Note

Apple cider is an unfiltered apple juice and can be found in the refrigerated section of most major supermarkets.

Freezer-Friendly

Wrap leftover slices in plastic wrap and freeze in a zip-top bag for up to 2 months.

Tahini Pumpkin Pie
Serves 8

It's not Thanksgiving without pumpkin pie, but getting that perfect consistency without evaporated milk can be a challenge. My solution: tahini! It's got just the right amount of fat to thicken the filling with a subtle sesame flavor. But that's just half the challenge! Making a flaky piecrust without butter or margarine (it's a no-no for me!) is not an easy feat, so I rely on my favorite nondairy fat: refined coconut oil. I like to freeze the coconut oil so that it incorporates into flaky bits inside the dough, and I add sesame seeds for an extra dose of nuttiness to pair with the filling. While untraditional, this elevated pumpkin pie is equally delicious and pairs wonderfully with my pomegranate-sumac cranberry sauce (see page 187).

CRUST

½ cup refined coconut oil, softened at room temperature

1¼ cups all-purpose flour, plus more for rolling

1 tablespoon sugar

½ teaspoon kosher salt

3 tablespoons raw sesame seeds, plus 1 tablespoon for topping

6 to 8 tablespoons ice water

1 egg, beaten

FILLING

1 (15-ounce) can pumpkin (not pumpkin pie filling)

3 extra-large eggs

½ cup creamy unsweetened nondairy milk, such as almond or oat milk

¼ cup tahini paste

½ cup (loosely packed) dark brown sugar

½ teaspoon ground cinnamon

½ teaspoon kosher salt

¼ teaspoon ground nutmeg

¼ teaspoon ground cloves

¼ teaspoon ground ginger

¼ teaspoon freshly ground black pepper

1. To prepare the crust: Spread the coconut oil in one layer on a piece of wax paper and freeze for 15 minutes, or until solid.

2. In a large bowl, whisk together the flour, sugar, salt, and 3 tablespoons sesame seeds until combined. Remove the coconut oil from the freezer, break it into shards, and add to the bowl. Use your fingers to cut in the coconut oil until it is the size of peas. Make a well in the center of the flour mixture and add 6 tablespoons of the ice water. Using a wooden spoon, mix the water into the flour until just combined. If the dough seems dry, add more water, a tablespoon at a time. Press the dough together, form into a disc, and wrap in plastic wrap. Chill the dough in the refrigerator for 1 hour (or up to overnight) or freeze for 20 minutes.

3. Preheat the oven to 375°F.

4. To prepare the filling: In a large bowl, whisk together the canned pumpkin, eggs, milk, tahini, brown sugar, cinnamon, salt, nutmeg, cloves, ginger, and pepper until smooth and creamy.

5. Remove the pie dough from the fridge. On a lightly floured work surface, roll the dough out into a 12-inch circle. Make sure to turn the dough about a quarter turn after every few rolls so you get an even thickness. Carefully place the dough into a 9-inch pie dish, pressing the dough into the bottom and sides of the dish. Trim any overhanging dough with a knife and

crimp the edges with a fork or flute the edges with your fingers, if desired.

6. Pour the pumpkin filling into the piecrust and transfer to a sheet tray. Brush the exposed pie dough with egg and sprinkle with sesame seeds. Bake for 40 to 50 minutes, or until the pumpkin filling is just set (it shouldn't jiggle). Cool and refrigerate for at least 3 hours before serving.

7. Cover any leftovers tightly with foil and store in the refrigerator for up to 5 days.

Easy Does It!
Use a frozen piecrust instead of making your own.

Freezer-Friendly
To freeze, wrap in two layers of plastic wrap and freeze for up to 2 months.

Cinnamon Babka Straws

Makes 24 straws

When my first cookbook, *Millennial Kosher*, came out in April 2018, my babka straws stole the show. In no time, my inbox was flooded with hundreds of photos of babka straws. I was spellbound! I've been getting requests for a cinnamon version ever since, and it's finally here! And just to make it *extra*, you've got not one but three topping choices!

CINNAMON FILLING

1 cup (packed) dark brown sugar
¼ cup canola oil
2 tablespoons all-purpose flour
1½ tablespoons ground cinnamon
2 tablespoons hot water
¼ teaspoon kosher salt

CRUMB TOPPING (OPTIONAL)

½ cup (packed) dark brown sugar
½ cup all-purpose flour
½ teaspoon ground cinnamon
¼ cup canola oil
1 teaspoon pure vanilla extract
¼ teaspoon kosher salt

BABKA TWISTS

2 sheets frozen puff pastry, thawed (Pepperidge Farm recommended)
1 extra-large egg plus 1 tablespoon water, beaten, for egg wash

CREAM CHEESE GLAZE (OPTIONAL)

1 cup confectioners sugar
4 ounces cream cheese, softened
4 tablespoons unsalted butter, softened
¼ cup whole milk
1 teaspoon pure vanilla extract

SIMPLE ICING (OPTIONAL)

2 cups confectioners sugar
2 to 4 tablespoons milk (any variety) or water
1 teaspoon pure vanilla extract

1. Preheat the oven to 375°F. Line two baking sheets with parchment paper.

2. To make the cinnamon filling: In a small bowl, combine the brown sugar, oil, flour, cinnamon, water, and salt.

3. If making the crumb topping option: In a second small bowl, combine the brown sugar, flour, cinnamon, oil, vanilla, and salt. Mix with a fork until coarse crumbs form.

4. To make the babka twists: Working with one sheet of puff pastry at a time, lightly roll out the dough to form a 10 × 12-inch rectangle. With the short side facing you, spread half of the cinnamon filling on the lower half of the dough with a knife. From the short side, fold the uncoated half of the dough over the coated side.

5. Using a pizza cutter or sharp knife, cut the pastry into 1-inch-thick strips. Transfer each strip to one of the baking sheets, spaced an inch or so apart. As you set them down, twist the ends in opposite directions a few times, lightly stretching the dough as you twist, to give the straws a spiraled look. Refrigerate the straws for 10 minutes. While they are chilling, repeat with the second sheet of puff pastry and the remaining cinnamon filling. Refrigerate the second sheet when it's ready.

6. Remove the baking pans from the fridge. Brush the straws with the egg wash and sprinkle with the crumbs (if using). If you prefer the cream cheese or sugar glaze, omit the crumbs. Bake for 20 minutes, or until puffed and golden.

RECIPE CONTINUES

7. If making one of the glazes, make them now. To make the cream cheese glaze, in a medium bowl using an electric mixer on medium speed, beat together the confectioners sugar, cream cheese, butter, milk, and vanilla until smooth and creamy.

8. To make the icing: In a medium bowl using a spoon, mix together the confectioners sugar, milk, and vanilla until smooth, adding more milk if needed.

9. Drizzle the desired glaze over the straws once they've cooled.

Note

When working with puff pastry, it's best to move quickly so the puff pastry doesn't get too soft and difficult to handle. If needed, place in the refrigerator for 10 minutes to firm up before twisting.

Freezer-Friendly

You can freeze the babka straws before baking (do not egg wash) and store them in a zip-top freezer bag for up to 2 months. Transfer the frozen straws to the baking sheet, brush with egg wash, and bake until puffed and golden. Alternatively, freeze after baking. Thaw and rewarm in the oven at 350°F for 6 to 8 minutes to crisp up before serving.

Peach Cornmeal Crisp

Serves 8

When it comes to fruit crisps, it's summer over winter for me. I love playing around with different seasonal fruits to create a bubbly crisp or cobbler for dessert, but stone fruits are my jam (pun intended!). You can use peaches, plums, or cherries for this crisp. Just sweeten it to taste depending on the tartness of your fruit. The cornmeal in the crisp topping adds a wonderful texture and color to the crisp that just screams summer, and paired with ice cream, it's a decadent dessert worthy of your BBQ feasts.

2½ pounds peaches (5 medium), halved, pitted, and sliced ¼ inch thick (do not peel)

⅓ cup plus 1 tablespoon (packed) dark brown sugar, divided

2 tablespoons bourbon

1 tablespoon cornstarch

½ teaspoon freshly squeezed lemon juice

¾ teaspoon kosher salt, divided

¾ cup all-purpose flour

½ cup yellow cornmeal

⅓ cup refined coconut oil, softened

¼ cup granulated sugar

Vanilla ice cream, for serving

1. Preheat the oven to 375°F.

2. In a large bowl, toss the peaches with ⅓ cup of the brown sugar, the bourbon, cornstarch, lemon juice, and ¼ teaspoon of the salt. Place the peaches into an 7 x 11-inch baking dish.

3. In a medium bowl, combine the flour, cornmeal, coconut oil, granulated sugar, remaining 1 tablespoon brown sugar, and remaining ½ teaspoon salt. Mix with your fingers to form crumbs and sprinkle over the peaches.

4. Bake for 45 to 50 minutes, until the fruit is bubbling and the topping is crisp and lightly browned. Remove from the oven and cool for 10 minutes before serving warm with ice cream.

5. Cover leftovers with foil and refrigerate (it may turn soggy).

Brownie Bar Hamantaschen
Makes 24 hamantaschen

When I was growing up, Reisman's brownie bars were my absolute favorite pastry. Imagine a Fig Newton, only stuffed with brownie instead of figs, coated in chocolate drizzle. That stuff was my kryptonite, and now it can be yours, too, in hamantaschen form!

HAMANTASCHEN DOUGH
½ cup canola oil
½ cup sugar
2 extra-large eggs
½ teaspoon pure vanilla extract
2 cups all-purpose flour, plus more for dusting
½ teaspoon baking powder
¼ teaspoon kosher salt

BROWNIE FILLING
½ cup sugar
¼ cup canola oil
1 large egg
½ teaspoon pure vanilla extract
½ cup all-purpose flour
¼ cup Dutch-processed cocoa powder
1 tablespoon instant espresso powder
⅛ teaspoon kosher salt

CHOCOLATE DRIZZLE
½ cup semisweet chocolate chips
1 tablespoon refined coconut oil

1. Preheat the oven to 350°F. Line two baking sheets with parchment paper.

2. To make the hamantaschen dough: In a large bowl, combine the oil, sugar, eggs, and vanilla and whisk until smooth. In a separate medium bowl, combine the flour, baking powder, and salt. Add the dry ingredients to the wet ingredients and stir until a smooth dough is formed. Wrap the dough in plastic wrap and refrigerate while you prepare the filling.

3. To make the brownie filling: Using the same wet and dry bowls you used for the hamantaschen dough, combine the sugar, oil, egg, and vanilla in the wet bowl and whisk until smooth. In the dry bowl, combine the flour, cocoa powder, espresso powder, and salt. Add the dry ingredients to the wet ingredients and stir until smooth.

4. Remove the hamantaschen dough from the fridge. On a lightly floured surface, roll out the dough ¼ inch thick. Cut circles out of the dough using a 2½-inch cookie cutter or a glass cup. Reroll the scraps and cut circles until you use up all the dough.

5. Place 1 teaspoon of the brownie filling in the center of each of the dough circles. Fold in the dough from three sides, pinching the corners to seal, leaving a small opening over the filling in the middle. Transfer the hamantaschen to the baking sheet and bake for 10 to 12 minutes, until the bottoms are lightly golden. Transfer the hamantaschen to a wire rack to cool.

6. To make the chocolate drizzle: Melt the chocolate chips in the microwave in 15-second increments or over a double boiler for 5 minutes, stirring until smooth. Stir in the coconut oil until melted and combined. Drizzle the chocolate over the hamantaschen and set aside for 20 minutes, until the chocolate sets.

Freezer-Friendly
To freeze, transfer to a zip-top bag and freeze for up to 2 months.

Malabi Pavlova

Serves 6

Pavlova is a dessert made of a meringue base that is crisp on the outside and soft and marshmallowy on the inside. It's topped with seasonal fruit and whipped cream. This version was inspired by one of my favorite Middle Eastern desserts, malabi, an orange blossom or rosewater-scented milky pudding topped with shredded coconut, chopped nuts, rose petals, and cinnamon.

6 large egg whites
1 teaspoon freshly squeezed lemon juice
1 teaspoon cornstarch
½ teaspoon pure vanilla extract
1½ cups granulated sugar
1 (14-ounce) can full-fat unsweetened coconut milk, refrigerated overnight
3 tablespoons confectioners sugar
1 teaspoon orange blossom water

For topping: Pomegranate seeds, shelled pistachios, rose petals, shredded coconut, and fresh fruit such as quartered figs or fresh berries

1. Preheat the oven to 250°F. Line a baking sheet with parchment paper.

2. In a large bowl, using a hand beater or the whisk attachment of a stand mixer, beat the egg whites on medium speed for 3 minutes, or until foamy. Add the lemon juice, cornstarch, and vanilla and continue to beat until incorporated.

3. Slowly add the granulated sugar in a steady stream for 2 minutes, or until fully incorporated. Increase the mixer speed to high and continue to beat the mixture another 3 to 5 minutes, until it is smooth and glossy and stiff peaks form. Feel the mixture between your fingers to ensure that the sugar has fully dissolved.

4. Using a spoon, create six free-form nests of the meringue mixture on the baking sheet, using the back of the spoon to make an indentation in the center of each mound. Transfer the baking sheet to the oven and bake for 90 minutes, until the meringues are firm and dry to the touch but not browned. Turn the oven off and allow the meringues to cool completely in the oven for 1 hour.

5. Clean out the bowl of your stand mixer and dry well. Carefully, without shaking it, remove the can of coconut milk from the refrigerator. Open the can and use a spoon to scoop out the thick layer of coconut cream from the top of the can (or use a can of coconut cream). Transfer the coconut cream to the bowl of the stand mixer. (Discard the coconut water that settled to the bottom of the can or add it to your morning smoothie!) Add the confectioners sugar and whisk together on medium speed for 2 to 3 minutes, until the cream becomes light and fluffy and small peaks form. Add the orange blossom water and beat to combine.

6. When ready to serve, top each pavlova with a generous dollop of coconut whipped cream and decorate with fruit and malabi toppings.

7. Store the unfilled meringues in an airtight container in a cool, dry place for up to 2 weeks or freeze for up to 1 month. Thaw at room temperature before serving. Refrigerate the coconut cream for 1 week or freeze for up to 1 month.

Variation

You can also make one large pavlova instead of individual ones. Serve on a cake stand in the center of the table.

Freezer-Friendly

Hawaij Gingersnaps

Makes 18 cookies

Sweet hawaij is the gingerbread spice of Yemenite cuisine. Its savory counterpart, Hawaij for Soup (page 304), is probably my favorite spice blend of all time. The sweet version, made with cardamom, ginger, cinnamon, allspice, and cloves, is traditionally called "hawaij for coffee" and works well in baked goods. Since silan, or date honey, has a rich molasses color and flavor (make sure you use 100 percent date syrup and not one that's been watered down with glucose syrup!), it gives these cookies their deep color and chewy bite.

2 cups all-purpose flour

1 recipe Hawaij for Coffee (page 304)

2 teaspoons baking soda

¼ teaspoon kosher salt

¾ cup canola oil

¼ cup granulated sugar

½ cup (packed) dark brown sugar

⅓ cup silan (100 percent date honey with no sugar added)

1 extra-large egg

⅓ cup turbinado sugar

1. Preheat the oven to 350°F. Line two baking sheets with parchment paper.

2. In a medium bowl, whisk together the flour, hawaij, baking soda, and salt until combined.

3. In a large bowl, whisk together the canola oil, granulated sugar, brown sugar, silan, and egg until creamy. Add the dry ingredients to the wet ingredients and use a spoon to mix until a smooth dough forms.

4. Use a 2-tablespoon scoop to measure out the dough and roll it gently into balls. In a small bowl, roll the cookie dough in the turbinado sugar until fully coated.

5. Place each sugar-coated cookie 2 inches apart on the prepared baking sheets. Bake for 10 minutes, until crisp. Transfer the cookies to a baking rack and cool completely before serving.

6. To freeze, transfer the cookies to a zip-top bag and freeze for up to 2 months.

Freezer-Friendly

Melinda's Olive Oil Cupcakes
Makes 15 cupcakes

I'm lucky enough to spend every Thanksgiving with my family at my friend Melinda's house. She prepares the most showstopping spread you have ever seen! One year, she put these olive oil cupcakes on the dessert buffet, and I could not get over how moist they were. Even my kids loved them! We've been making them ever since.

4 extra-large eggs

½ cup granulated sugar

½ cup honey

½ cup extra-virgin olive oil

¼ cup plus 2 tablespoons freshly squeezed orange juice (from 1 to 2 oranges), divided

2 tablespoons plus ¼ teaspoon orange zest (from about 3 oranges), divided

1½ cups all-purpose flour

1 tablespoon baking powder

1 teaspoon ground cardamom

½ teaspoon kosher salt

1 cup confectioners sugar

1. Preheat the oven to 350°F. Line three cupcake tins with liners for 15 cupcakes and grease with cooking spray.

2. In the bowl of a stand mixer with the whisk attachment, beat the eggs, granulated sugar, and honey together on medium speed for 2 minutes, until the color lightens to a pale yellow and the mixture is fluffy. With the mixer running on low, drizzle in the olive oil and ¼ cup of the orange juice until combined. Add 2 tablespoons of the orange zest and mix until incorporated.

3. In a medium bowl, whisk together the flour, baking powder, cardamom, and salt. Add the dry mixture to the wet mixture in the stand mixer and blend at medium speed until smooth. Pour the batter into the cupcake liners, filling them each three-quarters full.

4. Bake the cupcakes for 18 to 20 minutes, until a toothpick inserted comes out clean. Set the cupcakes aside to cool.

5. In a small bowl, whisk together the confectioners sugar, the remaining 2 tablespoons orange juice, and the remaining ¼ teaspoon orange zest. When the cupcakes are cool, spread the icing over the top of the cupcakes.

Variations

- *For a seasonal Chanukah dessert, I use this recipe to prepare an upside-down persimmon cake. Line a 9-inch cake pan with parchment paper and drizzle with ¼ cup honey. Arrange about 4 thinly sliced and peeled ripe Fuyu persimmons on the parchment in an overlapping pattern. Cover with the olive oil batter and bake at 350°F for 35 minutes, or until a toothpick inserted comes out clean. Flip the cake over and rest until serving. Serve with orange blossom coconut whipped cream (see page 253), crushed pistachios, and rose petals.*
- *You can also make this recipe with a mix of orange, lime, and grapefruit juices and zest. Use 2 teaspoons of each citrus zest and combine the juices together, using ¼ cup of the mixed juice instead of orange juice.*

Freezer-Friendly
Store the cupcakes in the freezer without the glaze in zip-top bags for up to 2 months.

Charoset Bars

Serves 12

Charoset is a relish made of fruit, nuts, and red wine that represents the mortar used by Jewish slaves in the building of pyramids in Egypt. It is one of the symbolic foods on the Passover seder plate, and its ingredients vary by custom. Sephardic charoset incorporates dried fruit (like dates, raisins, apricots, or figs), nuts (often almonds or walnuts), and cinnamon. Ashkenazi charoset includes fresh fruit (my dad always used pears, but apples are also common), walnuts, and red wine. This recipe fuses both versions into delicious bars that are so good, it's hard to imagine that they are kosher for Passover!

3 cups superfine blanched almond flour

¾ cup sugar

½ cup walnut or grapeseed oil

1 extra-large egg

1½ teaspoons kosher salt, divided

1 ripe pear or Granny Smith apple, peeled, cored, and roughly chopped

14 plump medjool dates, pitted (about 10 ounces)

¼ cup dry red wine

⅛ teaspoon ground cinnamon

½ cup chopped walnuts (about 2 ounces)

1. Preheat the oven to 350°F. Line an 8 × 8-inch pan with parchment paper.

2. In a medium bowl, stir together the almond flour, sugar, oil, egg, and 1 teaspoon of the salt until combined into a smooth dough. Remove 1 cup of the dough and set aside.

3. Using your hands, press the remaining dough into the bottom of the prepared pan in an even layer. Bake for 12 minutes, until lightly puffed. Cool for 5 minutes.

4. In the bowl of a food processor fitted with the S blade, pulse together the pear, dates, wine, cinnamon, and remaining ½ teaspoon salt until pasty, scraping down the sides of the bowl with a rubber spatula as needed (it should resemble mortar, just like the story of the Exodus!).

5. Add the walnuts to the reserved 1 cup of dough and mix with your fingers to combine. Spread the charoset filling over the cooled baked dough and crumble the walnut mixture over the top. Bake for 18 minutes, until browned around the edges. Set the bars aside to cool and cut into squares. Store in an airtight container (use parchment paper if layering) at room temperature for up to 2 days or refrigerate for up to a week.

Freezer-Friendly
To freeze, wrap squares individually in plastic wrap, transfer to a zip-top bag, and freeze for up to 2 months.

Rainbow Cookie Mandelbroit

Makes 2 rolls, 12 cookies per roll

Unlike crispy, twice-baked biscotti, old-school mandelbroit is baked once and has a soft texture that lends itself well to this rainbow cookie–inspired variation that is everything you love about the three-layer radioactive cake, minus all the work. If you really want to doll them up, feel free to dip in chocolate and add colorful sprinkles!

2 cups all-purpose flour

1 cup superfine blanched almond flour

1 cup sugar

1 teaspoon baking powder

½ teaspoon kosher salt

1 cup canola oil

3 extra-large eggs, beaten

2 tablespoons pure almond extract

½ teaspoon pure vanilla extract

½ cup blanched slivered almonds

½ cup diced Turkish dried apricots

½ cup semisweet chocolate chips

Red and green gel food coloring, about
    ¼ teaspoon each

1. Preheat the oven to 350°F. Line two baking sheets with parchment paper.

2. In a large bowl, combine the flours, sugar, baking powder, and salt, making sure to break up any clumps of almond flour. In a small bowl, combine the oil, eggs, almond extract, and vanilla. Add the wet ingredients to the dry ingredients and mix with a spoon until a creamy dough forms. Add the almonds and apricots and stir to combine.

3. In separate small bowls, divide the dough into three equal portions. Add green food coloring to the first portion and red to the second portion, mixing with your hands until incorporated. Leave the third portion plain. (The dough will be sticky.)

4. Use half of each portion of dough so that you have red, plain, and green to form a log that is 15 inches long and 6 inches wide. Use wet hands to form each ball of dough into a 2-inch-thick strip, placing them alongside each other so that they touch and lightly press the dough together to adhere. Repeat with the remaining pieces of dough on the other sheet pan.

5. Bake the loaves for 25 minutes, alternating the trays halfway through, until puffed and lightly browned on the bottom. Cool for 10 minutes and then use a sharp knife to slice them into 1-inch slices.

Freezer-Friendly

To freeze, wrap the mandelbroit in parchment paper and transfer to a zip-top bag. Freeze for up to 2 months.

"As Easy as Pie" Blueberry Pie Cake

Makes 2 pie cakes, serves 8 per pie

If there's one recipe that makes me think of my bubby, it's her blueberry pie cake made with a simple oil-based dough that comes together with a spoon and simple store-bought canned blueberry pie filling. Come Friday afternoon, our family Whatsapps are often filled with photos of this cake, fresh out of the oven. As Bubby would say, "It's as easy as pie!"

3 cups all-purpose flour

1 cup granulated sugar

1 tablespoon baking powder

½ teaspoon kosher salt (my addition!)

¾ cup canola oil

3 extra-large eggs, beaten

1 teaspoon pure vanilla extract

1 (21-ounce) can blueberry pie filling

1 egg plus 1 tablespoon water, beaten, for egg wash (optional)

3 tablespoons turbinado sugar, for topping (optional)

1. Preheat the oven to 350°F. Grease two 9-inch round cake pans with cooking spray.

2. In a large bowl, whisk together the flour, granulated sugar, baking powder, and salt. Then add the canola oil, eggs, and vanilla. Mix with a spoon until a creamy dough forms, kneading lightly with your hands, if needed, until it comes together. Freeze the dough for 20 minutes.

3. Remove the dough from the freezer and divide it in two. Working with one batch at a time, place half of the dough on the bottom of the pan, spreading it out into a thin layer over the bottom and around the sides. Top with half of the pie filling. Divide the remaining half of the dough into 6 balls, roll them into strips on a piece of parchment paper and form a lattice over the pie filling by placing 3 strips in one direction and 3 in the opposite direction (that's how my bubby would do it!). Alternatively, use a rolling pin to roll out the dough on a lightly floured surface and cut ¾-inch strips to create the lattice, weaving perpendicular strips of dough under and over each other (that's how

my food stylist, Chaya, did it!). Repeat with the remaining ingredients to make the second pie. Brush the strips with the egg wash and sprinkle with turbinado sugar.

4. Bake the pies for approximately 45 minutes, until they are golden and starting to brown.

Variation

You can use any canned pie filling of your choice, including cherry, apple, strawberry, or peach, or use multiple flavors, dividing the fillings into sections on top of the pie dough before topping it with the lattice.

Note

If you prefer to make your own blueberry pie filling from scratch, place 4 cups blueberries, 1 cup granulated sugar, ¾ cup water, and 1 tablespoon lemon juice in a large saucepan. Heat over medium heat and cook, stirring occasionally, until you notice some of the blueberries breaking down, for 3 minutes. Mix ¼ cup cornstarch with ¼ cup water in a small bowl and stir until smooth. Stir in the cornstarch slurry and whisk continuously until thickened, for 2 minutes.

Freezer-Friendly

To freeze, wrap the pie in a layer of parchment paper and foil and freeze for up to 2 months.

Gluten-Free Chocolate Chip Scones

Makes 8 scones

I don't have much of a sweet tooth, so rich and decadent desserts are not really my thing, even though I love making them for everyone else! But scones? Scones I can get behind. They're not too sweet, and just a dab of butter or jam make them perfect for afternoon tea or dessert. The fact that they're gluten free is just a bonus—perfect for Passover breakfast!

2½ cups superfine blanched almond flour
½ cup arrowroot flour
½ cup coconut flour
2 teaspoons baking powder
2 tablespoons granulated sugar
¾ teaspoon kosher salt
½ cup melted refined coconut oil
½ cup honey
1 extra-large egg
1 teaspoon pure vanilla extract
⅓ cup canned full-fat coconut milk
¾ cup semisweet chocolate chips
1 egg plus 1 tablespoon water, beaten, for egg wash
1 tablespoon Demerara sugar

1. Preheat the oven to 350°F. Line a baking sheet with parchment paper.

2. In a large bowl, whisk together the almond flour, arrowroot flour, coconut flour, baking powder, granulated sugar, and salt. In a medium bowl, whisk together the coconut oil, honey, egg, vanilla, and coconut milk. Add the wet ingredients to the dry and stir with a wooden spoon until a smooth dough forms. Gently fold in the chocolate chips until evenly dispersed.

3. Form the dough into a 9-inch-diameter disc and cut it into 8 triangles. Transfer the scones to the prepared baking sheet, spacing them apart. Brush with the egg wash and sprinkle them with Demerara sugar. Bake for 20 minutes, or until the bottoms of the scones are lightly golden and the tops are crisped.

4. Store in an airtight container at room temperature for up to 3 days or freeze in a zip-top bag for up to 2 months.

Freezer-Friendly

Noshes & Nibbles

Mango Paletas with Mexican Sweet and Sour Candy Spice

Makes 8 popsicles, depending on size

On one of my food crawls of Miami, I was hopping from one restaurant to the next when I passed a kosher paletas shop. Paletas are Mexican popsicles made from natural fruits. I chose the sweet and tart mango pop, and what came next totally revolutionized my popsicle experience: Miguelito candy chile powder. Like Tajín, a popular Mexican chili-lime seasoning, Miguelito is tangy and spicy but also contains sugar. It's like a popsicle coated in sour sticks, and once you try it, you'll never go back to plain old popsicles again!

MANGO PALETAS

16 ounces frozen mango chunks
½ cup canned full-fat coconut milk
2 tablespoons freshly squeezed lime juice
¼ cup honey

SWEET & SOUR CANDY SPICE

2 tablespoons sugar
2 teaspoons citric acid (also called sour salt)
½ teaspoon cayenne pepper
¼ teaspoon kosher salt

1. To make the mango paletas: In a blender, combine the mango chunks, coconut milk, lime juice, and honey until smooth and creamy. Transfer the mixture to a popsicle mold and add a popsicle stick to each popsicle. Freeze for 4 hours, or until solid.

2. To prepare the sweet & sour spice: In a small bowl, combine the sugar, citric acid, cayenne, and salt.

3. When ready to serve, remove the mango pops from the mold and dip in the candy spice.

Easy Does It!

Use Tajín or chili lime seasoning in place of sweet-and-sour candy spice, and mix in some granulated sugar if you'd like.

Variation

For a crunchier topping, use turbinado sugar in place of the granulated sugar. You can also swirl some full-fat coconut milk into the popsicles, if desired.

Make it a cocktail!

Dip your cocktail glass in lime juice and sweet-and-sour candy spice. Mix 1 cup mango juice with 1 ounce lime juice, 1½ ounces tequila, ½ ounce triple sec, and 1 tablespoon agave; shake and pour over ice.

Marzipan Butter Cups

Makes 10 cups

Step aside peanut butter cups, there's a new cup in town, and it's my all-time favorite Passover treat—MARZIPAN! I love how easy it is to make at home, and it's so versatile too! Add chunks to cookies, brownies, or ice cream, or just roll it into balls and decorate to your liking. But pretty please, only use PURE almond extract and not imitation, which has an artificial taste. It makes all the difference!

¾ cup blanched almond meal or flour (see Note)
½ cup plus 2 tablespoons confectioners sugar, plus more as needed
Pinch of fine sea salt
1 teaspoon pure almond extract
10 ounces semisweet chocolate chips
Maldon sea salt flakes, for finishing (optional)

1. In the bowl of a food processor fitted with the S blade, pulse the almond meal, confectioners sugar, and fine sea salt until the ingredients are combined. Add 1 tablespoon water and the almond extract and blend until a paste forms and starts to pull away from the sides of the bowl. If the paste is very sticky, add more confectioners sugar so that it forms a dough and doesn't stick to your fingers.

2. Place the marzipan in the center of a 10-inch-long piece of plastic wrap and roll into a log shape that's about 5 inches long. Roll the log in the plastic and twist the ends to seal. Roll back and forth on a work surface a few times to make the log evenly round. Freeze about 1 hour, or until firm.

3. In a microwave-safe bowl, melt the chocolate chips, stirring every 15 seconds, until smooth, or melt in a zip-top bag using my hack on page 19.

4. Set ten paper cupcake liners on a baking sheet. Pour a heaping tablespoon of the melted chocolate into each cupcake liner and spread it out to evenly cover the bottom. Bang the baking sheet on your work surface to evenly disperse the chocolate.

5. Remove the marzipan from the freezer and slice it into 10 rounds. They should be the same diameter as the cupcake liner; if they are smaller, flatten them with your hand to fit. Place the marzipan on top of the chocolate layer and cover it with another heaping tablespoon of chocolate. Bang the baking sheet on your work surface again to evenly coat the marzipan in the chocolate.

6. Sprinkle the cups with Maldon sea salt (if desired) and freeze the cups for 30 minutes, or until solid. Store in an airtight container in the fridge for up to 1 week or freeze for up to 2 months.

Note

If you don't have almond meal or flour, you can create your own by pulsing 1 cup of blanched slivered almonds in the food processor until finely ground—take care to stop before you turn the almonds into almond butter!

Freezer-Friendly

Candied Pecans, Two Ways

If you stop at any candy stall in the Machane Yehuda Shuk in Jerusalem, you'll find an assortment of candied nuts, especially pecans. Many cafés in Israel even offer a candied pecan milkshake on the menu. These halva pecans were inspired by a similar version I tried there, which I adapted in countless ways, including this speculoos version! They're great for snacking, gift giving, or adorning a cheese board.

CANDIED HALVA PECANS
Makes 2 cups

2 tablespoons refined coconut oil
2 tablespoons silan (date honey)
2 tablespoons sugar
1 teaspoon kosher salt
8 ounces raw pecans (about 2 cups)
2 tablespoons raw sesame seeds
1 cup shredded halva (available in Middle Eastern markets)

1. Preheat the oven to 350°F. Line a baking sheet with parchment paper.

2. In a small saucepan over medium heat, combine the coconut oil, silan, sugar, and salt. Bring the mixture to a simmer, whisking constantly, 2 to 3 minutes, until it starts to bubble, and blend into a homogenous dark caramel. Remove the caramel from the heat and stir in the pecans and sesame seeds.

3. Spread the pecans on the prepared baking sheet and bake for 12 to 15 minutes, stirring halfway through with a silicone spatula, until toasted and caramelized.

4. Remove the nuts from the oven and, using a silicone spatula, immediately stir in the shredded halva until evenly coated. Cool completely at room temperature for at least 4 hours, until crispy.

5. Store the pecans in an airtight container at room temperature for up to 2 weeks.

SPECULOOS PECANS
Makes 2 cups

3 tablespoons refined coconut oil
3 tablespoons maple syrup
3 tablespoons (packed) dark brown sugar
1 teaspoon kosher salt
¼ teaspoon ground cinnamon
8 ounces raw pecans (about 2 cups)
15 Lotus Biscoff brand cookies, finely crushed into crumbs

1. Preheat the oven to 350°F. Line a baking sheet with parchment paper.

2. In a small saucepan over medium heat, combine the coconut oil, maple syrup, brown sugar, salt, and cinnamon. Bring the mixture to a simmer, whisking constantly, 2 to 3 minutes, until it starts to bubble into a homogenous dark caramel. Remove the caramel from the heat and stir in the pecans.

3. Spread the pecans on the prepared baking sheet and bake for 20 minutes, stirring halfway through with a silicone spatula, until toasted and caramelized. Remove the pecans from the oven and immediately stir in the cookie crumbs until the pecans are evenly coated. Cool completely at room temperature for at least 4 hours, until crispy.

4. Store the pecans in an airtight container at room temperature for up to 2 weeks.

BBQ Bissli
Serves 10

They always say that chefs enjoy the simplest foods at home. A chef friend of mine eats cereal and milk most nights for dinner, while another crushes on good old grilled cheese made with American cheese and ketchup (!). I'm no chef, but as someone who works in food, I can totally relate to this. My lazy late-night eats? Pasta with tuna and ketchup (don't @ me!) or a bag of BBQ Bissli (an Israeli crunchy wheat snack that comes in an assortment of shapes with a variety of savory flavors) when I have the munchies. And if you want to chef it up, you can make your own! My kids rated these better than the original!

16 ounces rotini pasta
2 tablespoons nutritional yeast
2 tablespoons granulated garlic
4 teaspoons granulated onion
4 teaspoons smoked paprika
2 teaspoons chili powder
3 teaspoons sugar
2½ teaspoons kosher salt
1 teaspoon ground turmeric
2½ cups canola oil

1. In a large pot of salted water over high heat, cook the rotini for 6 minutes, or a little more than half of the cooking time given on the package. Drain the pasta and spread it on a kitchen towel to dry for 10 minutes.

2. In a medium bowl, combine the nutritional yeast, garlic, onion, paprika, chili powder, sugar, salt, and turmeric and stir until blended.

3. Line a plate with paper towels. In a heavy-bottomed saucepan, heat the canola oil until it registers 375°F on a deep-fry thermometer. Deep-fry the pasta in batches, stirring the pasta as soon as you add it to the oil so it doesn't stick. Fry for 3 minutes, or until golden brown. Remove the pasta from the oil with a slotted spoon or spider, quickly drain it on the prepared plate, and toss it into the seasoning. Transfer to a large bowl and repeat with the remaining pasta.

4. Cool the bissli completely before transferring it to an airtight container. Store at room temperature for up to 2 weeks.

Note

This spice blend's nacho-like flavor is also delicious over roasted cauliflower or broccoli, potatoes, and popcorn.

Honey Mustard and Onion Pretzels

Serves 10

What do you do with bottom-of-the-bag leftover bits and pieces of pretzels? Make the best sweet-and-salty finger-licking snack ever! Of course now, since we love these so much, I make them using a fresh bag of whole pretzels.

½ cup extra-light olive oil or grapeseed oil

¼ cup honey

3 tablespoons yellow mustard

2 teaspoons onion powder

1 teaspoon garlic powder

½ teaspoon dried oregano

12 ounces sourdough hard pretzels, broken apart into bite-size pieces

1. Preheat the oven to 275°F. Line a baking sheet with parchment paper.

2. In a large bowl, combine the olive oil, honey, mustard, onion powder, garlic powder, and oregano. Add the pretzels to the bowl and toss well to coat.

3. Transfer the pretzels onto the baking sheet and spread them out in an even layer. Bake for 45 minutes, stirring every 15 minutes, until the sauce is fully absorbed and the pretzels are crispy.

4. Cool completely for 1 hour, then store in an airtight container at room temperature for up to 2 weeks.

Quinoa Cracklings
Makes 8 servings

Gimme all the savory snacks! Chocolate is great, but I love to nosh on umami treats, and these salty, crispy shards of Parmesan plus quinoa make a great nibble for parties or on-the-go snacking. They also make for a great salad topper.

½ cup uncooked quinoa
1¼ cups shredded Parmesan cheese
½ teaspoon dried oregano
½ teaspoon dried basil
½ teaspoon garlic powder
Pinch of red pepper flakes (optional)

1. In a small saucepan, combine the quinoa with ¾ cup water. Bring to a boil over medium-high heat, reduce to a simmer, and cook, covered, for 10 minutes, until all the liquid is absorbed. Remove the quinoa from the heat and continue to steam, covered, for 5 minutes, until fluffy.

2. Spread the quinoa on a parchment-lined baking sheet and let cool slightly while you preheat the oven to 400°F.

3. Add the Parmesan, oregano, basil, garlic powder, and red pepper flakes (if using) to the quinoa. Use a silicone spatula to fold everything together until combined, then spread the quinoa evenly on the tray. Bake for 10 to 15 minutes, until the Parmesan is melted and starting to brown around the edges. Remove from the oven and cool completely before breaking apart into 2-inch shards.

4. Store at room temperature in an airtight container for up to 1 week.

Variation

Experiment with different flavorings such as za'atar, herbes de Provence, lemon zest, dried rosemary, or whatever you like.

Pineapple Teriyaki Beef Jerky

Serves 6

Jerky is all the rage these days, and believe it or not, it's fairly simple to make. You don't even need a dehydrator! Every time I make these, the entire batch is gone in minutes, so you might want to double the recipe.

1 pound top of the rib roast or London broil cut from the shoulder

½ cup pure unsweetened pineapple juice

¼ cup (packed) dark brown sugar

3 tablespoons sambal oelek or chili garlic sauce (see Note)

3 tablespoons soy sauce

1 tablespoon freshly grated ginger using a rasp-style grater

1 tablespoon toasted sesame oil

1. Place the roast in the freezer for 1 hour, then slice crosswise and against the grain into ¼-inch-thick slices. (Alternatively, ask your butcher to "slice the meat for jerky" for you.)

2. In a gallon-size zip-top bag, combine the pineapple juice, brown sugar, sambal oelek, soy sauce, ginger, and sesame oil. Add the meat to the bag and refrigerate overnight.

3. The next day, preheat the oven to 185°F. Line a baking sheet with foil and place a wire baking rack on top.

4. Remove the meat from the marinade and discard the remaining marinade. Spread the meat on the prepared baking rack so it all lies flat. Bake for 3 to 4 hours, flipping the meat over halfway through cooking, until the meat is fully dehydrated. (If the meat is not fully dehydrated after 4 hours, keep cooking it until it is fully dried. It shouldn't be wet or sticky.)

5. Remove the meat from the rack. Store in an airtight container in the fridge for up to 1 week.

Note

Sambal oelek is a Southeast Asian chili sauce. You can find it near the soy sauce in most grocery stores. Huy Fong Foods is a popular kosher brand. If you can't find their sambal, use their chili garlic sauce instead.

Peanut Butter Pretzel Bombs

Makes 12 bombs

Frozen dates are a revelation! You will always find some in my freezer. I fill them with tahini, nut butter, chestnut cream, Nutella—you name it! And for topping—sesame seeds, crumbled Lotus Biscoff cookies, cocoa nibs, nuts, and always a pinch of Maldon sea salt flakes because I love salty-sweet. Here, pretzels offer the crunch and pair especially well with the peanut butter.

1 cup semisweet chocolate chips

1 tablespoon refined coconut oil

12 plump medjool dates (about 9 ounces)

¼ cup natural peanut butter (smooth or chunky, your choice)

½ cup pretzels, finely crushed

Maldon sea salt flakes, for finishing

1. In a small microwave-safe bowl, melt the chocolate chips and the coconut oil in 15-second increments, stirring between each, until completely melted and smooth. Or in a double boiler over medium heat, melt the chocolate chips, stirring until smooth. Stir in the coconut oil until combined.

2. Line a baking sheet with parchment paper. Cut a slit in each date and remove the pits. Using a spoon, fill each date with about 1 teaspoon of the peanut butter. Using a fork, dip the dates into the melted chocolate and transfer them to the baking sheet. Quickly sprinkle them with the crushed pretzels and Maldon sea salt.

Freezer-Friendly

Transfer the baking sheet to the freezer and freeze for 20 minutes, or until the chocolate hardens. Store in an airtight container in the freezer for up to 2 months.

Poppy Seed and Onion Kichel
Makes 8 to 10 servings

In upstate New York, you'll find pletzel, or onion boards (an onion poppy-seed focaccia), at every kosher bakery and supermarket. Growing up, it was part and parcel of our summer diet—alongside Kool-Aid and Creamsicles! There is one bakery that sells poppy seed and onion kichel, a cracker version of the pletzel, and I always beeline to the far corner of the bakery to grab a bag. This gluten-free version is Passover-and diet-friendly, and you can sub in your favorite flavors like za'atar, Everything Bagel Spice (page 305), or assorted seeds to customize it to your taste.

3 tablespoons extra-virgin olive oil
1 large Spanish onion, finely diced
Kosher salt
1½ cups super-fine blanched almond flour
1 teaspoon poppy seeds
1 extra-large egg, lightly beaten

1. Preheat the oven to 350°F.

2. In a medium skillet over medium-high heat, heat the olive oil. Add the onion and sauté for 20 minutes, stirring often, or until deeply caramelized. Season with a pinch of salt.

3. In a small bowl, stir together the almond flour, poppy seeds, and ¼ teaspoon salt to combine.

4. Add the beaten egg to the almond flour mixture, mixing with a spoon until a dough forms (it will be a little sticky). Add half of the onions and continue to mix to incorporate.

5. Place the dough between two sheets of parchment paper, 18 inches long, and use a rolling pin to roll it out until you have a very thin layer, about ⅛ inch thick. Remove the top sheet of parchment and spread the remaining onions over the dough. Cover with the parchment paper again and press down with a rolling pin just enough for the onions to adhere to the dough.

6. Peel off the top layer of parchment paper. Cut the dough into rustic squares, roughly 2 × 2 inches (I like to use a pizza wheel for this). Use the edges of the parchment to transfer the kichel to a baking sheet.

7. Bake for 15 to 20 minutes, until lightly browned and crisp. Remove the pan from the oven and cool the crackers completely before breaking them apart. Store in an airtight container at room temperature for up to 1 week or freeze the baked crackers for up to 2 months.

Variations

Omit onion and poppy seeds and use these fillers instead:

- *For seeded crackers, add ⅓ cup mixed seeds (such as sesame, pumpkin, sunflower, and flax).*

- *For za'atar crackers, add 2 tablespoons za'atar and 3 tablespoons sesame seeds.*

- *For everything bagel crackers, add ⅓ cup Everything Bagel Spice (page 305).*

Freezer-Friendly

The Apfelbomb

Makes 1 cocktail

Call me "old fashioned" (my favorite cocktail!), but I'm a whiskey girl at heart, with bourbon being my spirit of choice. Here, I put an autumnal spin on the classic drink, with notes of apple cider and maple. For a lighter cocktail, double the apple cider and divide between two glasses.

1½ ounces (3 tablespoons) apple cider

1½ ounces (3 tablespoons) bourbon

½ ounce (1 tablespoon) triple sec or freshly squeezed orange juice

1 ounce (2 tablespoons) freshly squeezed lemon juice

½ ounce (1 tablespoon) maple syrup

Splash of ginger beer

Thinly sliced apple and cinnamon stick, for garnish

1. In a cocktail shaker, combine the apple cider, bourbon, triple sec, lemon juice, and maple syrup. Fill the shaker with ice, cover, and shake vigorously until the outside of the shaker is very cold.

2. Using a cocktail strainer or slotted spoon to hold back the ice, pour the drink into a rocks glass filled with more ice. Top off with the ginger beer and garnish with an apple slice and cinnamon stick.

White Russian Shakerato

Makes 1 cocktail

A highlight from a recent gastronomic tour of Rome was the shakerato at Roscioli. The drink is essentially an espresso, shaken with sugar in a cocktail shaker to create a luxurious foam without any milk, served in a cocktail glass dusted with cocoa powder. Of course, they've been doing this long before espresso martinis went viral on social media! I took the concept to the next level by making a White Russian–inspired cocktail out of it. It makes for an incredible after-dinner drink (yes, you can use decaf espresso too)!

1 shot espresso, or 1½ ounces (3 tablespoons) water plus 1 tablespoon instant espresso

½ ounce (1 tablespoon) coffee liqueur, such as Misceo

½ ounce (1 tablespoon) vodka

1½ teaspoons sugar

2 tablespoons half-and-half, or to taste

Dutch-processed cocoa powder, for dusting

1. In a cocktail shaker, combine the espresso, coffee liqueur, vodka, and sugar. Fill the shaker with ice, cover, and shake vigorously until the outside of the shaker is very cold and the drink is very frothy.

2. Using a cocktail strainer or slotted spoon to hold back the ice, pour the drink into a champagne coupe glass. Top with half-and-half. Dust with cocoa powder before serving.

Gelt Glogg

Serves 4 to 6

Glogg is Swedish spiced mulled wine, usually served in the winter around the holidays, and poured over blanched almonds and raisins. Since I always have lots of chocolate gelt around the house during the holidays, I thought; What if I poured the wine over chocolate gelt? And Gelt Glogg was born.

1 (750ml) bottle dry red wine, such as cabernet sauvignon, merlot, pinot noir, or petite syrah

1 cup (packed) dark brown sugar

¼ cup bourbon

7 cardamom pods

5 whole cloves

3 strips orange peel

2-inch piece fresh ginger, peeled and sliced lengthwise

2 cinnamon sticks

Bittersweet chocolate gelt

1. In a medium saucepan over low heat, combine the red wine, brown sugar, bourbon, cardamom pods, cloves, orange peel, ginger, and cinnamon sticks. Bring the mixture to a bare simmer (so as not to cook out the alcohol) and stir to dissolve the sugar. Remove from the heat and steep for 1 hour.

2. When ready to serve, strain the wine through a fine-mesh sieve (or skim using a strainer) to remove the whole spices and return the wine to the saucepan. Bring the wine back to a bare simmer over low heat.

3. Add a piece of chocolate gelt to the bottom of a hot toddy cup and pour the warm wine over it. Serve warm with cinnamon sticks to stir in the chocolate.

You're So Extra!

Toppings, Dressings, Dips, Salsas,
Spreads & Spices

TOPPINGS

CANDIED JALAPEÑOS

Makes 1 (16-ounce) jar

We are legitimately obsessed with Trader Joe's Hot & Sweet Jalapeños in my house. The jar doesn't even last us through the week. I even use the brine in my salad dressings and sauces! I won't call this a copycat version, but it's definitely a good effort! Chile de árbol is a small spicy Mexican chile pepper you can find in most major supermarkets.

2 cups sugar
⅔ cup distilled white vinegar
1 teaspoon kosher salt
5 jalapeños, thinly sliced
1 teaspoon minced garlic flakes
1 dried chile de árbol (optional)

1. In a small saucepan over medium heat, combine the sugar, vinegar, salt, and ½ cup water and bring to a boil. Remove from the heat and add the jalapeños.

2. Transfer the jalapeños and brining liquid to a 16-ounce jar. Add the garlic flakes and dried chile (if using). Refrigerate for up to 1 month.

POMEGRANATE PICKLED ONIONS

Makes 2 cups

Pickled onions are always the answer to "what's missing" on a sandwich. Or a taco. Or a grain bowl. They're tangy and crunchy and a little bit sweet—the perfect condiment! To switch things up a bit, I use pomegranate juice as the base of the brine and sweeten it with honey for a change.

½ cup red wine vinegar
½ cup pomegranate juice
3 tablespoons honey
1½ teaspoons kosher salt
1 small red onion, thinly sliced into half-moons

1. In a 1-quart pot over medium-high heat, combine the vinegar, pomegranate juice, honey, and salt and bring to a boil. Stir and remove from the heat. Add the sliced onions and set aside to cool.

2. Once cooled, transfer the onion and pickling liquid to a 16-ounce jar and refrigerate for up to 1 month.

3. Add to fish tacos, burgers, hot dogs, pulled beef sandwiches, grilled cheese, and salads.

PISTACHIO DUKKAH

Makes 1¼ cups

Dukkah is a rough-textured and crunchy Egyptian nut, seed, and spice blend that is traditionally used as a dip with olive oil and bread. It's usually a combination of whatever nuts and seeds the cook has around the kitchen, so feel free to adjust this recipe to what you have on hand.

½ cup shelled raw pistachios
¼ cup raw sesame seeds
2 tablespoons coriander seeds
2 tablespoons cumin seeds
1 teaspoon dried thyme
1 teaspoon kosher salt

1. Preheat the oven to 350°F. Line a small baking sheet with parchment paper.

2. On the prepared baking sheet, mix together the pistachios, sesame seeds, coriander seeds, and cumin seeds and bake for 10 minutes, until toasted and fragrant.

3. In a food processor fitted with the S blade or spice grinder, combine the nuts and seeds with the thyme and salt and pulse until coarsely chopped.

4. Store in an airtight container at room temperature for up to 2 months.

5. Sprinkle over avocado toast, yogurt, tahini, hummus, salad, eggs, rice, or roasted vegetables or mix into panko bread crumbs for a flavorful breading.

HARD-BOILED EGGS

Place the eggs in a small saucepan and cover completely with cold water. Bring to a boil over medium-high heat, cover the pot, and turn off the heat. Let the eggs sit, covered, for 12 minutes. Drain the eggs and run under cold water to halt the cooking.

JAMMY SOFT-BOILED EGGS

If there was one hashtag to define my favorite food choice, it would be #putaneggonit. That's me! I love a runny or jammy yolk, and when marinated in a soy marinade, it makes for a special treat on its own.

1. In a medium bowl, combine ice and water and set aside.

2. In a 1-quart saucepan over high heat, bring 3 cups water to a boil. Using a slotted spoon, slowly add the eggs to the water and reduce the heat to medium. Cook the eggs for 6½ minutes exactly, then use a slotted spoon to remove the eggs from the pot and transfer them to the ice water for 2 minutes, until cool enough to peel. Peel and serve.

SOY-MARINATED EGGS

1 cup boiling water
⅔ cup soy sauce
⅓ cup mirin
2 tablespoons unseasoned rice vinegar
¼ cup (packed) dark brown sugar
Pinch of red pepper flakes
6 soft-boiled eggs

Optional additions: sliced ginger, sliced garlic, sliced Thai red chile pepper, sliced scallions, roasted sesame seeds

1. In a 6 x 6-inch container (6 cups or 1½ quarts), combine the boiling water, soy sauce, mirin, rice vinegar, brown sugar, red pepper flakes, and any optional additions and stir to dissolve the brown sugar.

2. Place the peeled soft-boiled eggs in the marinade, cover, and refrigerate for 2 to 6 hours, until the eggs turn brown. (If needed, place a plate over the eggs to ensure that they are fully submerged in the marinade.) The longer they sit, the more flavorful they become. I don't recommend marinating for more than 12 hours however, because the eggs will turn rubbery.

3. Remove the eggs from the marinade (discard or reserve to marinate another batch of eggs; you can use it two more times) and serve over ramen, stir-fries, avocado toast, pasta, or rice.

Tip
For best results, use older eggs—they peel more easily!

CHILI CRISP

Makes 2 cups

If there's one recipe that you make in this book that's a little out of your comfort zone, MAKE IT THIS ONE! I've seen chili crisp around forever, but there has never been a kosher version on the market (at least not at the time of writing this book!), so I was determined to make it happen. Chili crisp is aptly named for the crunchy slices of garlic and shallots in the sauce, but this Chinese condiment has endless variations. What they all have in common is a textural component (think dried onions, garlic, nuts, sesame seeds, etc.), chile flakes (from Korean, Chinese, Mexican, Indian chiles, etc.), aromatics (cardamom, cinnamon, star anise, ginger, cumin, Sichuan peppercorns, etc.), and oil (any neutral-flavored oil with a high smoke point like canola, avocado, peanut, grapeseed, etc.). The oil is heated and poured over the chiles and aromatics to activate them. You can play around with different combinations to suit your taste. Here, I add garlic, shallots, umami spice, cashews, and soy sauce for an addictive umami flavor and supreme crunch.

3 green cardamom pods
1 cinnamon stick
12 garlic cloves, thinly sliced (about ½ cup)
4 small shallots, thinly sliced into rounds (about 1½ cups)
1½ cups grapeseed oil
½ cup roasted cashews, roughly chopped
¼ cup red chile flakes (see Note)
½ teaspoon umami spice or dried mushroom powder
1 tablespoon soy sauce
1 teaspoon sugar
½ teaspoon kosher salt

1. In a medium saucepan, cover the cardamom pods, cinnamon stick, garlic, and shallots with oil. Cook the mixture over medium heat for 20 to 25 minutes, stirring occasionally (the perimeter of the pan will start to darken first, so you need to keep it moving), until the shallots and garlic crisp up and turn a golden color.

2. While the shallots and garlic are cooking, in a medium glass bowl, combine the cashews, red pepper flakes, and umami spice.

3. Remove the cardamom and cinnamon stick from the oil and pour the hot oil into the bowl over the cashew mixture and stir. Add the soy sauce, sugar, and salt and stir to combine.

4. Let the chili crisp cool before transferring it to an airtight container. Store in the refrigerator for up to 1 month.

Note

To make the chile flakes, buy dried unsmoked red chiles from the international aisle of your local grocery (many are kosher-certified). I used a combination of Aleppo and kashmiri chiles, both mild chile peppers, and I removed the seeds before grinding for less heat. In general, the larger the chiles, the less heat they have. After removing the stems and seeds (if desired), simply pulse in a food processor or spice grinder until flaky.

CRISPY TORTILLA STRIPS

Soft corn tortillas > hard-shell tortillas, always! Which pretty much leaves me with leftover corn tortillas in my fridge most of the time ... which is how I got the idea to home-fry these awesome crunchy toppers for soup, salad, or guacamole.

RECIPE CONTINUES

Canola oil, for frying
Corn tortillas, cut into ½-inch-wide strips
Kosher salt to taste
Chili powder to taste (optional)

1. In a large skillet, heat 2 inches of oil to 350°F. Line a plate with paper towels.

2. Working in batches, add a handful of tortilla strips at a time to the oil, giving it a quick stir, and fry for 3 minutes, or until golden.

3. Use a slotted spoon or spider to remove the tortillas from the oil and drain the strips on the prepared plate. Sprinkle with salt and chili powder (if desired). Store in a zip-top bag for up to 2 weeks.

Variations

- *Sprinkle with Cinnamon-Sugar (page 305) instead of chili powder and use as a topping for ice cream!*

- *To bake the strips (which are not nearly as good!), spread the tortilla strips in a single layer on a greased parchment-lined baking sheet and spray generously with cooking spray. Bake at 425°F for 8 to 10 minutes, turning halfway through, until golden brown and crisp.*

TOGARASHI SEASONING

Togarashi is the name of a Japanese chile pepper, but it also refers to the seven-spice blend, shichimi togarashi, that is like the Japanese version of everything bagel spice. It's sprinkled on everything from rice to eggs, noodles, and fries. In my version, I use dried red pepper flakes and black pepper, but if you can source ichimi togarashi (spicy Japanese chili powder) and sanshō pepper (Japanese peppers that have a mild numbing feel on the tongue), feel free to swap them in (they're pretty easy to find online). I like adding it to mayo to make a flavorful spicy mayo spread.

½ sheet nori seaweed
1 tablespoon toasted sesame seeds
2 teaspoons dried orange zest
1½ teaspoons red pepper flakes

1 teaspoon poppy seeds
½ teaspoon coarsely ground black pepper
¼ teaspoon ground ginger

1. Toast the nori by holding it with tongs over a low flame for a few seconds. In a food processor fitted with the S blade or spice grinder, coarsely grind the nori, or crumble it with your hands.

2. In a small bowl, combine the nori flakes, sesame seeds, orange zest, red pepper flakes, poppy seeds, black pepper, and ground ginger and toss until evenly distributed.

3. Store the seasoning in an airtight container at room temperature for up to 2 months.

4. Sprinkle the seasoning over ramen, sushi rice, soup, popcorn, roasted cabbage, kale chips, avocado toast, and eggs.

FESTIVE EVERYTHING BAGEL SALAD CRISPS

These fun wonton crisps are a must-have for your next holiday party! I use cookie cutters to stamp shapes from the wrappers—for Chanukah, I use a menorah or dreidel cutter, for Rosh Hashanah I use apple- or shofar-shaped cutters, and for birthdays I'll use initials or numbers. The crisps are a fantastic stand-in for bread-y croutons—feel free to use any spices of your choice such as flaky salt, za'atar, or sesame seeds.

1 package eggroll or wonton wrappers
1 extra-large egg white
Everything Bagel Spice (page 305)

1. Preheat the oven to 400°F. Cut shapes out of the wonton wrappers using cookie cutters of your choice. Place on a parchment-lined baking sheet that is greased with cooking spray.

2. Brush the cutouts with the egg white and sprinkle with everything bagel spice. Spray with cooking spray. Bake for 5 to 6 minutes, or until browned and crisp.

DRESSINGS

PICKLE BRINE CAESAR

Makes 1 cup

¾ cup mayonnaise
3 tablespoons pickle brine
1 garlic clove, minced
1 tablespoon Dijon mustard
Kosher salt and freshly ground black pepper
   to taste

In a medium bowl, whisk together the mayonnaise, brine, garlic, Dijon, capers, salt, and pepper until creamy.

Serve over iceberg wedges, massage into kale, or toss with romaine lettuce.

Note

Depending on the acidity of your pickle brine, you may need to add a bit of sweetener to taste.

POMEGRANATE MOLASSES DRESSING

Makes ½ cup

¼ cup grapeseed oil or light olive oil
3 tablespoons pomegranate molasses
2 tablespoons freshly squeezed lemon juice
½ teaspoon ground sumac
2 tablespoons honey
2 teaspoons Dijon mustard
1 teaspoon kosher salt
½ teaspoon freshly ground black pepper

In a medium bowl, whisk together the oil, molasses, lemon juice, sumac, honey, Dijon, salt, and pepper until creamy.

Serve with arugula or spring mix salad greens topped with roasted beets, sweet potatoes, apples, or pears, add pomegranate seeds and toasted nuts or seeds.

ALMOND BUTTER DRESSING

Makes ½ cup

Soy- and peanut-free, allergy friendly, and kosher for Passover!

2 garlic cloves
1½-inch piece of fresh ginger, peeled and
   roughly chopped
½ Thai red chile pepper, seeds and veins
   removed, roughly chopped, or ½ teaspoon
   red pepper flakes
1 tablespoon freshly squeezed lime juice
¼ cup creamy almond butter
3 tablespoons coconut milk
½ teaspoon kosher salt

Place the garlic and ginger in the bowl of a food processor fitted with the S blade and blend until finely minced. Add the chile, lime juice, almond butter, coconut milk, and salt and blend until creamy.

Use as a vegetable dip, drizzle over smashed or spiralized cucumbers, mix into slaw, or toss with pasta.

ZA'ATAR GARLIC DRESSING

Makes 1 cup

⅔ cup olive oil
⅓ cup freshly squeezed lemon juice
1 teaspoon kosher salt
½ teaspoon freshly ground black pepper
2 tablespoons za'atar
2 cloves garlic, minced
1 tablespoon honey

In a small bowl, and whisk together the oil, lemon juice, salt, pepper, za'atar, garlic, and honey.

Toss over a fresh vegetable salad.

DIPS, SALSAS & SPREADS

TOGARASHI AIOLI
Makes 1 cup

1 cup mayonnaise
1 tablespoon Togarashi Seasoning (page 296)
1 tablespoon unseasoned rice vinegar
1 teaspoon toasted sesame oil
1 teaspoon sriracha

In a medium bowl, combine the mayonnaise, togarashi seasoning, rice vinegar, sesame oil, and sriracha. Store in an airtight container in the fridge for up to 2 weeks.

Use the togarashi aioli as you would use any spicy mayo—in a sandwich, as a dip for fish, or as a dressing for sushi salad.

Easy Does It!
For a simple spicy mayo, combine 1 cup mayonnaise, 2 tablespoons unseasoned rice vinegar, 3 tablespoons sriracha, and 2 teaspoons toasted sesame oil.

CHIPOTLE AIOLI
Makes 1 cup

1 cup mayonnaise
1 chipotle chile pepper in adobo, seeds removed
1 tablespoon adobo sauce
2 garlic cloves
1 tablespoon freshly squeezed lime juice
½ teaspoon smoked paprika
Kosher salt to taste

In the bowl of a food processor fitted with the S blade, purée the mayonnaise, chipotle pepper, adobo sauce, garlic, lime juice, paprika, and salt until smooth. Transfer to an airtight container and refrigerate for up to 2 weeks.

Add to burgers and tacos, use as a crudités dip, or slather over grilled corn.

TOMATO OLIVE SALSA
Serves 6

1 pint grape tomatoes, quartered
1 cup thinly sliced pimiento-stuffed olives
1 small red onion, finely diced
2 tablespoons extra-virgin olive oil
1 tablespoon freshly squeezed lemon juice
1 teaspoon dried oregano
Kosher salt and freshly ground black pepper
    to taste

In a medium bowl, stir together the tomatoes, olives, onion, oil, lemon juice, oregano, salt, and pepper. While best served fresh, you can store leftovers in an airtight container in the fridge for up to 2 days.

Serve with scrambled eggs, roasted fish or chicken, tacos, and beans.

SUNDRIED TOMATO TAPENADE
Makes ½ cup

⅓ cup sundried tomatoes packed in extra-virgin
    olive oil
2 garlic cloves
½ cup fresh flat-leaf parsley
Zest and juice of ½ lemon
3 tablespoons extra-virgin olive oil from the
    sundried tomatoes (or use regular extra-
    virgin olive oil if you don't have enough)
2 tablespoons drained capers
Kosher salt and freshly ground black pepper
    to taste

In the bowl of a food processor fitted with the S blade, pulse the sundried tomatoes, garlic, parsley, lemon zest and juice, olive oil, capers, salt, and pepper until very finely chopped. Transfer to an airtight container and refrigerate for up to 2 weeks.

Serve with roasted fish, grilled chicken, on a cheese or charcuterie board, or in a deli or tuna sandwich.

Variation

Omit the capers and add ½ cup chopped marinated artichokes or sliced kalamata olives. Use basil in place of parsley.

CHIMICHURRI

Makes ¾ cup

1 cup (packed) fresh parsley, cilantro, or a mix
½ cup extra-virgin olive oil
2 scallions (white and green parts), ends trimmed
Juice of 1 lime
2 garlic cloves
2 tablespoons red wine vinegar
1 teaspoon dried oregano
½ teaspoon red pepper flakes
Kosher salt and freshly ground black pepper to taste

In the bowl of a food processor fitted with the S blade, blend the parsley, olive oil, scallions, lime juice, garlic, vinegar, oregano, red pepper flakes, salt, and pepper until smooth.

Serve with grilled chicken or meat, or mix with mayonnaise to make a dip or salad dressing (great with grilled chicken salad!).

EXTRA-CREAMY TAHINI

Makes ¾ cup

½ cup tahini paste (stir thoroughly before measuring)
1 garlic clove, minced
Juice of ½ lemon
¼ teaspoon ground cumin

⅓ cup ice water
Kosher salt to taste

In the bowl of a food processor fitted with the S blade, blend the tahini paste, garlic, lemon juice, and cumin. As you begin to blend and while the machine is running, slowly pour the ice water through the feed tube. Blend for a few minutes until extra smooth, fluffy, and silky. Season with salt and adjust as desired. Transfer to an airtight container and store in the refrigerator for up to 2 weeks.

Easy Does It!

For quick and easy tahini, just whisk the ingredients together until emulsified.

RESEK

Makes ½ cup

2 ripe plum tomatoes
Kosher salt to taste

In a medium bowl, using a box grater, grate the tomatoes against the medium hole side. Discard the peel. Season with salt, transfer to an airtight container, and store in the refrigerator for up to 1 week.

SCHUG

Makes 1 heaping cup

3 jalapeño peppers, deseeded and deveined (optional for less heat)
1 large bunch of fresh parsley, cilantro, or a mix (2 to 3 cups packed)
¼ cup extra-virgin olive oil
Juice of ½ lemon
4 garlic cloves

RECIPE CONTINUES

1 teaspoon ground cumin
Kosher salt to taste

In the bowl of a food processor fitted with the
S blade, pulse the jalapeños, parsley and/or
cilantro, olive oil, lemon juice, garlic, cumin, and
salt until finely chopped. Transfer to an airtight
container and store in the refrigerator for up to
1 week.

SMOKY HARISSA
Makes 2 cups

6 dried chiles de árbol
5 dried guajillo chiles
2 dried ancho chiles
¼ cup extra-virgin olive oil, plus more for
　finishing
3 garlic cloves
1 tablespoon freshly squeezed lemon juice
2 teaspoons tomato paste
1½ teaspoons kosher salt
1 teaspoon smoked paprika
1 teaspoon sweet paprika
1 teaspoon ground cumin
½ teaspoon ground coriander
1 to 2 teaspoons honey (optional)

In a medium bowl, soak the árbol, guajillo, and
ancho chiles in hot water for 30 minutes (use
a plate to keep them submerged, if needed).
Drain and discard the stems and seeds. In the
bowl of a food processor fitted with the S blade,
combine the chiles with the olive oil, garlic,
lemon juice, tomato paste, salt, smoked paprika,
sweet paprika, cumin, coriander, and honey (if
using). Blend until smooth. Transfer the harissa
to a glass jar and top with a thin layer of olive oil.
Refrigerate for up to 2 months.

Notes

- *You can find kosher dried chile peppers
  in the international aisle at most major
  supermarkets.*

- *For a less spicy harissa, reduce the chile
  de árbol.*

SPICE BLENDS

HAWAIJ FOR SOUP

1 tablespoon ground turmeric
1 tablespoon ground cumin
2½ teaspoons ground coriander
1½ teaspoons coarsely ground black pepper
1 teaspoon ground cardamom
¼ teaspoon ground cloves

In a small bowl, combine all the ingredients.
Store in an airtight container for up to 6 months.

HAWAIJ FOR COFFEE

1 tablespoon ground cardamom
2 teaspoons ground ginger
½ teaspoon ground cinnamon
¼ teaspoon ground allspice
¼ teaspoon ground cloves

In a small bowl, combine all the ingredients.
Store in an airtight container for up to 6 months.

HOUSE RUB

2 tablespoons ground coriander
1 teaspoon freshly ground black pepper
1 teaspoon granulated garlic
1 teaspoon onion powder
1 tablespoon (packed) dark brown sugar
2 teaspoons mustard powder
1 tablespoon smoked paprika
1½ teaspoons kosher salt

In a small bowl, combine all the ingredients.
Store in an airtight container for up to 6 months.

This all-purpose rub works great on brisket,
grilled chicken breasts, whole roasted chicken,
whole side of salmon, and fish tacos.

COFFEE RUB

2 tablespoons instant espresso
2 tablespoons (packed) dark brown sugar
1 tablespoon smoked paprika
1 tablespoon kosher salt
2 teaspoons chili powder
1 teaspoon freshly ground black pepper
1 teaspoon garlic powder
1 teaspoon onion powder
¼ teaspoon cayenne pepper

In a small bowl, combine all the ingredients.
Store in an airtight container for up to 6 months.

This rub works well on grilled and roasted
meats. Drizzle with maple syrup toward the end
of cooking for a sweet finish!

GARAM MASALA

1½ tablespoons ground cardamom
1 tablespoon ground cumin
2 teaspoons ground coriander
1 teaspoon ground cinnamon
1½ teaspoons freshly ground black pepper
½ teaspoon ground cloves
½ teaspoon ground nutmeg

In a small bowl, combine all the ingredients.
Store in an airtight container for up to 6 months.

SHAWARMA SPICE

1 tablespoon ground cumin
1 tablespoon ground coriander
2 teaspoons paprika
1 teaspoon ground turmeric
½ teaspoon garlic powder
½ teaspoon ground allspice
¼ teaspoon ground cinnamon
¼ teaspoon freshly ground black pepper
½ teaspoon kosher salt

In a small bowl, combine all the ingredients. Store in an airtight container for up to 6 months.

EVERYTHING BAGEL SPICE

1 tablespoon poppy seeds
1 tablespoon toasted sesame seeds
1 tablespoon dried minced garlic flakes
1 tablespoon dried minced onion flakes
2 teaspoons kosher salt

In a small bowl, combine all the ingredients. Store in an airtight container for up to 6 months.

CINNAMON-SUGAR

¼ cup sugar
1 tablespoon ground cinnamon

In a small bowl, combine the ingredients. Store in an airtight container for up to 6 months.

Confit, x3!

Confit, a process of slow cooking food in fat for a buttery, melt-in-your-mouth texture, is all the rage. The hawaij garlic confit from my cookbook *Millennial Kosher* has stained many a tablecloth! Here are some favorites that I've been making since then; it's the only time you'll catch me splurging on pre-peeled garlic cloves! Serve confit warm as a dip for challah or sourdough bread or use as a topping for hummus or rice.

JALAPEÑO DATE CONFIT
Makes 3 cups

The sweet and spicy combo in this confit is addictive. Thank you to Chana Blumes for the recipe! (By way of @wukogals!)

2 leeks (white and pale green parts), washed
2 jalapeños, sliced ¼ inch thick
½ cup peeled garlic cloves
12 pitted medjool dates, roughly chopped
¾ teaspoon kosher salt
1½ cups extra virgin olive oil

Preheat the oven to 350°F. Cut the leek in half lengthwise and wash under running water to remove dirt. Pat dry and cut into ½-inch-thick slices. Transfer to a nonreactive baking dish, season with the salt, and add the olive oil until mostly covered. Bake, uncovered, for 45 minutes, or until buttery soft and starting to brown, stirring halfway through.

TOMATO LEMON CONFIT
Makes 2 cups

My go-to when I've got extra grape tomatoes lying around.

1 pint grape tomatoes
½ cup peeled garlic cloves
½ lemon, thinly sliced into half-moons
3 sprigs of fresh thyme, rosemary, or a mix
1 teaspoon balsamic vinegar
¼ teaspoon freshly ground black pepper
½ teaspoon kosher salt, or to taste
1 cup extra-virgin olive oil

Combine the tomatoes, garlic, lemon, thyme and/or rosemary, and vinegar in a nonreactive baking dish, season with salt, and add olive oil until mostly covered. Bake, uncovered, for 45 minutes, or until buttery soft and starting to brown, stirring halfway through.

CHICKPEA CONFIT
Makes 3 cups

Adapted from my food stylist Chaya Rappoport's recipe! She came up with the brilliant idea to confit chickpeas, and I'm all over it!

1 (14-ounce) can chickpeas, rinsed and drained
½ lemon, sliced
3 shallots, peeled and quartered
1 handful of fresh parsley
½ teaspoon smoked paprika
2 teaspoons Hawaij for Soup (page 304)
1 teaspoon kosher salt
¼ teaspoon freshly ground black pepper
1½ cups extra-virgin olive oil (enough to just cover the chickpeas)
Ground sumac, for topping

Preheat the oven to 350°F. Add the chickpeas to a nonreactive baking dish along with the lemon slices, shallots, parsley, paprika, Hawaij, salt, and pepper. Cover with olive oil and stir to combine. Bake, uncovered, for 40 to 50 minutes, stirring once or twice during cooking, until the shallots and lemon start to caramelize. Sprinkle with sumac before serving.

How to Plan Menus

Planning a menu is truly an art form, but it's one that can be learned, and it's an important one to master. Growing up in an orthodox Jewish family with Ashkenazi roots, there was always an overabundance of food. I'm passionate about changing the way we eat and serve because I want to take the pressure out of the kitchen and put the love back into it! Cooking should be fun, and feeding people should be an enjoyable experience for everyone—especially the cook. I'm also conscious of food costs and I never like to see anything go to waste, so I've mastered the art of a balanced meal.

In true Jewish mother form, scaling back on overfeeding is going to be hard at first, but I promise you no one is going to starve! A well-executed menu, with flavors that complement one another, is so much more pleasurable than serving a smorgasbord of dishes that don't work together. Taking the time to plate your food beautifully and set an elegant table with good wine and a nice ambiance (candles, cloth napkins, maybe a centerpiece of flowers) are all part and parcel of planning a meal.

Taking that all into consideration, what's in a menu? If you take a look at a typical restaurant menu, you'll find:

APPETIZER
finger food, small bites to be served hot or cold
Examples: nachos, tuna tartare, gefilte fish, dumplings, hummus with topping, salad

SOUP
optional but suggested for a festive meal
Examples: matzo ball soup, butternut squash soup, lentil soup

ENTRÉE
includes a protein, carb, and vegetable or salad
Examples: steak with sweet potato purée and arugula salad, chicken with couscous and cauliflower, fish and chips with roasted broccoli

DESSERT
There's always room for this course!
Examples: cake, pie, mousse, fresh fruit, sorbet

To tie a menu together, try sticking to a specific type of cuisine, such as Middle Eastern, Asian, or traditional Jewish foods. Most importantly, you can follow a recipe and plan a menu, but the real secret ingredient? It's love! Remember to have fun and enjoy the process. *It's just food.* And worst-case scenario: there's always takeout!

SAMPLE FRIDAY NIGHT SHABBAT MEAL

Appetizer: World Peace Challah (page 127), Simply Crudo with Cilantro Crema (page 150), Loaded Eggplant Carpaccio (page 101)

Soup: Moroccan Carrot Soup (page 115)

Entrée: Turkey Roast with Za'atar Gravy (page 172), Herbed Farro Pilaf (page 237), Roasted Beet and Citrus Salad (page 88)

Dessert: Baklava Palmiers (page 240), Halva Pecans (page 272)

RECIPES FOR JEWISH HOLIDAYS

SHABBAT: THE DAY OF REST

God created the world in six days and rested on the seventh, so from sundown on Friday evening until nightfall on Saturday night, I, along with others in the Jewish community, observe a day of rest. We celebrate with a festive Friday night dinner that often includes a fish, soup, and meat course followed by dessert. For Shabbat afternoon lunch, a fish course is traditionally served followed by a meat course that typically includes a stew that has simmered overnight.

World Peace Challah (page 127)

Golden Chicken Soup (page 131)

Cholent with Quick Kishke (page 134)

Deli Pinwheels (page 76)

Ma's Perfect Potato Kugel (page 133)

"As Easy as Pie" Blueberry Pie Cake (page 262)

ROSH HASHANAH: THE JEWISH NEW YEAR

New Year occurs in the fall and is celebrated by eating traditional foods called simanim to symbolize our hopes for a sweet new year. They include leeks, pomegranate, gourds (squash like acorn, butternut, delicata, kabocha, spaghetti, and pumpkin), dates, black-eyed peas (some use green beans), apples and honey, beets, carrots, and fish head (some use a ram's head).

Jeweled Hummus (page 50)

New Age Waldorf Salad (page 91)

Golden Milk Pumpkin Soup (page 107)

Cabbage and Apple Roast Chicken (page 165)

Harvest Bundt Cake (page 243)

YOM KIPPUR: DAY OF ATONEMENT

Yom Kippur occurs shortly after Rosh Hashana in the fall. It's a day for fasting and repentance, but to prepare ourselves, we have not one but two feasts on the eve of the fast. Dumplings, or kreplach, are a customary addition to the meal. The fast is followed by another meal to break the fast when it ends.

BEFORE THE FAST

Apple and Honey Mustard Salmon (page 143)

Simanim Potstickers with Pomegranate Dipping sauce (page 58)

Lemony Red Lentil Soup with Saffron (page 111)

Yemenite "Soup" Sheet Pan Chicken (page 158)

AFTER THE FAST

Pastrami-Style Gravlax (page 149)

Bougie Tuna Bagel (page 75)

Sabich Salad (page 98)

SUKKOT: THE FESTIVAL OF HUTS

During the harvest holiday of Succot, all meals are eaten outside in a sukkah (a temporary hut), commemorating the sheltering of the Jews in the desert when they left Egypt. Many festive meals are prepared during the holiday.

Bloody Mary Pickled Salmon (page 55)

Slow Cooker Berbere Brisket (page 188)

Orange Cardamom Rice (page 234)

Bubby's Stuffed Cabbage (page 136)

Corned Beef and Cabbage Ramen (page 119)

Rainbow Cookie Mandelbroit (page 261)

CHANUKAH: THE FESTIVAL OF LIGHTS

During the wintertime celebration of Chanukah, we light the menorah and eat foods that have been fried, like latkes and donuts, to commemorate the miracle of the small jug of oil that burned on the menorah in the Holy Temple for eight days and nights, after it's rededication by the Maccabees following it's desecration by the Greeks. It is also customary to eat dairy foods.

Fried Cornichons with Sweet Chili Dip (page 46)

Chestnut Latte Soup (page 116)

Sweet Noodle Kugel Latkes with Bourbon Raisin Jam (page 217)

Garlic Knot Crown with Brie and Tomato Jam (page 49)

Melinda's Olive Oil Cupcakes (page 257)

Gelt Glogg (page 288)

PURIM: THE HOLIDAY OF JOY

On Purim, we celebrate the victory of the Jews over the wicked Haman in the days of Queen Esther of Persia. We dress up in fun costumes, give food gifts to friends, eat hamantaschen, and make l'chaim over drinks.

Kishke Dogs (page 61)

Buffalo Hasselback Salami (page 65)

Nachos Bassar (page 62)

Chicken and "Waffle" Drumsticks with Hot Maple Syrup (page 164)

Brownie Bar Hamantaschen (page 250)

The Apfelbomb (page 284)

PASSOVER: THE HOLIDAY OF FREEDOM

In the spring, we celebrate Passover for eight days, commemorating the freedom of the Jews from slavery in Egypt. We don't eat any chametz (leavened grain). Matzo is a staple during the eight-day festival.

The Rebbetzin's Gefilte Fish (page 128)

Passover Panzanella with Matzo Brei Croutons (page 102)

Matzarayes (page 81)

Charoset Bars (page 258)

Marzipan Butter Cups (page 271)

Gluten-Free Chocolate Chip Scones (page 265)

SHAVUOT: THE FESTIVAL OF ROSES

Shavuot in May commemorates the giving of the Torah on Mount Sinai. Dairy foods are traditionally eaten, and we decorate our homes and synagogues with flowers.

Stuffed Branzino (page 140)

Arugula and Delicata Squash Salad with Feta (page 94)

Spinach Artichoke Khachapuri (page 208)

Leek and Corn Crustless Ricotta Quiche (page 210)

Malabi Pavlova (page 253)

Acknowledgments

If it takes a village to raise a child, it takes a community to birth a cookbook, and I have so many people who have held my hand along the way.

First and foremost, thank you to God for instilling in me the strength, passion, and drive to persevere despite many odds.

Thank you to my beautiful children, Chuma, Esther, Ari, Peretz, and Rosie. You are the greatest taste-testers, kitchen assistants, cleaner-uppers, cheerleaders, and snugglers. Everything I do, I do for you, and everything I've accomplished is because of you. You are my most cherished recipe.

To my mom, for being there through thick and thin, and my sister, Sara, for always having my back. To my brother, Mendy, for your wise advice and counsel.

To Adeena Sussman, this is all you, baby! For being my mentor, my greatest champion, and most of all, my friend.

To the friends and colleagues who supported me throughout this journey and beyond. There are no words to convey my gratitude in this space. I am forever grateful to Dina Gorodetsky, Rivka Wineberg, Chanchi and Chony Milecki, Mike Solomonov, Shushy Turin, Chaya Suri Leitner, Melinda Strauss, Jordana Hirschel, Jordana Kohn, Itta Werdiger, Rochel Leah Shapiro, Paula Shoyer, Danielle Renov, Naomi Nachman, Chana Blumes Geisinsky, Beth Warren, Baily Vogel, Lilly Eidelman, Levana Kirschenbaum, Leah Schapira.

To the incredible crew at Clarkson Potter, it was such an honor to work with every one of you! Raquel Pelzel, editor extraordinaire—for believing in me and my vision and for bringing it to life with so much integrity and respect, never missing a beat! Thank you, Bianca Cruz, for filling in all the gaps, and to Ian Dingman for your incredible talent in making this book as beautiful as it is.

To my styling dream team, Chaya Rappoport and Rachel Boardman, I could not have asked for a better pair to make each food photo picture-perfect and to celebrate over ice cream at the end of it. I love you ladies! Gefilte fish foodies forever!

Thank you to my agent, Stacey Glick, for being my literary Google and always being there to answer my questions.

To the talented Meir Kruter, for all your graphics and artistic assistance, and to Lauren Volo, for capturing my life behind the scenes so perfectly.

Thank you, Miriam Rosenthal, for organizing the recipe testing and to all of my amazing recipe testers who helped ensure that each recipe was perfect:

Tamar Abell, Sarah Abraham, Melissa Abu, Channah Akkerman, Chana Arnold, Nechama Bachrach, Deveaux Barron, Yakira Begun, Bella Benarroch, Esti Benchimol, Amanda Benishai, Francine Birk, Ruthie Bodner, Esther Braun, Shoshana Brody, Lauren Brookner, Tamar Burack, Jordana Cohen, Rebecca Cohen, Batsheva Dalezman, Fran Davids, Joyce Eisner, Barbara Engler, Sylvia Fallas, Jamie Feit, Robyn Feldberg, Pessy Florans, Hindy Garfinkel, Dani Geft, Aliza Getz, Eti Gipsman, Libby Goldberger, Tzivia Goldfein, Frimee Goldstein, Dina Gorodetsky, Miriam Gross, Esti Hamel, Sema Hammer, Aviva Hassan, Fraidy Hess, Katie Hoffman, Lori Huberfeld, Shira Huberfeld, Miriam Jacknis, Shira Kalish, Chaya Kibel, Sabrina Kudowitz, Sara Leibowitz, Rena Levy, Sarra Lorbert, Mushka Lowenstein, Shoshana Markowitz, Sruly Meyer, Martha Meyers, Anna Mogilevsky, Naomi Nachman, Batya Nadler, Dina Nathanson, Mushka Novack, Bina Oscherowitz, Heidi Pollicove, Sara Popper, Sarah Rabinowitz, Brittany Ray, Joy Resmovits, Yael Rosen, Esti Rosenblatt, Faigy Rosenblatt, Mimi Samet, Raizy Sandel, Melissa Schon, Rivka Schusterman, Sori Schwartz, Jan Shapiro, Kate Shur, Jason Sigal, Michelle Singer, Dina Spivak, Melinda Strauss, Shoshana Sturm, Stefanie Sturm, Yitzi Taber, Shushy Turin, Miriam Vogel, Liora Wittlin, Tova Zafrany, and Henny Zolty.

Special thanks to Seth Leavitt @abelesheymann, Shmayie Friedman @carvingblockmeats, Gourmet Glatt Boro Park @gourmetglattbp, Wood & Stone @woodandstonebrooklyn, Staub @staub_usa, Fortessa @fortessatableware, and Smithey Ironware Co @smitheyironware.

As the Hebrew saying goes, "The last is the most cherished." I am especially grateful for the longtime readers, fans, and followers of *Busy in Brooklyn*, who feed my foodie fire and who have loved and supported me throughout this journey. You inspire me.

Index

Page numbers in *italics* indicate photos.

Copyright © 2023 by Chanie Apfelbaum
Photographs Copyright © 2023 by Chanie Apfelbaum
All rights reserved.

Published in the United States by Clarkson Potter/Publishers, an imprint of Random House, a division of Penguin Random House LLC, New York.
ClarksonPotter.com
RandomHouseBooks.com

CLARKSON POTTER is a trademark and POTTER with colophon is a registered trademark of Penguin Random House LLC.

Library of Congress Cataloging-in-Publication Data
Names: Apfelbaum, Chanie, author.
Title: Totally kosher / by Chanie Apfelbaum.
Description: New York : Clarkson Potter, [2023] | Includes index.
Identifiers: LCCN 2022020787 (print) | LCCN 2022020788 (ebook) | ISBN 9780593232613 (hardcover) | ISBN 9780593232620 (ebook)
Subjects: LCSH: Jewish cooking. | Kosher food. | LCGFT: Cookbooks.
Classification: LCC TX724 .A67 2023 (print) | LCC TX724 (ebook) | DDC 641.5/676--dc23/eng/20220503
LC record available at https://lccn.loc.gov/2022020787
LC ebook record available at https://lccn.loc.gov/2022020788

ISBN 978-0-593-23261-3
eISBN 978-0-593-23262-0

Photographer: Chanie Apfelbaum
Lifestyle Photographers: Lauren Volo and Naftali Marasow
Production Assistant: Rachel Boardman
Recipe Developer: Chanie Apfelbaum
Food Stylist: Chaya Rappoport

Editor: Raquel Pelzel
Editorial Assistant: Bianca Cruz
Production Editor: Serena Wang
Production Manager: Heather Williamson
Compositors: Merri Ann Morrell, Hannah Hunt, and Nick Patton
Copy Editor: Hope Clarke
Indexer: Jay Kreider
Marketer: Chloe Aryeh
Publicist: Erica Gelbard
Book and cover design by: Ian Dingman
Cover photographs by: Chanie Apfelbaum

Printed in China

10 9 8 7 6 5 4 3 2 1

First Edition